DOWN AND UNDER

Dave Hadfield

DOWN AND UNDER

A Rugby League
Walkabout In Australia

Scratching Shed Publishing Ltd

First published by Scratching Shed Publishing Ltd in 2009
Registered in England & Wales No. 6588772.
Registered office:
47 Street Lane, Leeds, West Yorkshire. LS8 1AP

www.scratchingshedpublishing.co.uk

ISBN 978-0956007575

Unless stated otherwise, all photographs are by Dave Woods
& Dave Williams - www.rlphotos.com

A catalogue record for this book is available from the British Library.

Typeset in Warnock Pro Semi Bold and Palatino

Printed and bound in the United Kingdom by
L.P.P.S.Ltd, Wellingborough, Northants, NN8 3PJ

To Ruth, for putting up with my absence and,
even worse, my presence

And in memory of Dave Topliss,
who would never, ever have let bad rugby spoil a good trip

Contents

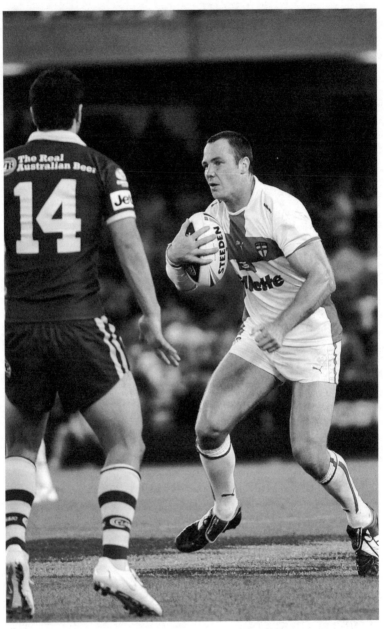

Adrian Morley in action for England

FOREWORD
by ADRIAN MORLEY
Warrington & England

I've known Dave Hadfield for many years now, and that's hugely depressing.

Not depressing knowing Dave, but depressing because the length of time that I've known him means I am in the twilight of my career in this, the greatest game of all.

I have always found Dave's writing on the game to be knowledgeable, funny and nostalgic. This is a man who you can tell has a passion for rugby league and genuinely loves everything about it.

For someone to walk the length of the country to every rugby league ground in England as Dave did in *Up and Over*, well, you know that he means business.

Dave and I found we had something in common when he was writing an early profile on me and I happened to mention that Bob Dylan was my favourite artist. That was it for the next hour or so, as we discussed our favourite albums and songs.

Down And Under

I envy the fact that he was even at the famous Free Trade Hall concert in Manchester in 1966 – the one where someone in the audience yelled 'Judas', although Dave assures me it wasn't him.

We've shared a few beers on more than one occasion on both sides of the world. Whether back home at a few watering holes in Salford or in the sun at my adopted home in Sydney, I always find him great company.

The first time I went to Australia myself was as a 19-year-old with the Great Britain nines squad. The tournament was held in Townsville, North Queensland, in mid-January, the middle of the Aussie summer.

I loved it from the start. The first few days were spent snorkelling on the Great Barrier Reef and visiting an Australian wildlife zoo. Coming from Salford and only having ever been on a few holidays around Europe, Oz was like another world.

In my naivety I just presumed that all of Australia was tropical, extremely hot and not as built up as back home. It wasn't until I had a chat with our coach, Andy Gregory, that he educated me on where we were geographically and why it was so bloody hot and that Sydney was the Mecca of rugby league down under. I put Sydney on my 'cities to visit' list right there and then.

I went back to Australia later that year during the ill-fated World Club Championship, when we visited Adelaide this time, and Townsville again. As things turned out, I didn't get to Sydney until after the 1999 Tri-Nations, when I spent three weeks not doing a great deal except soaking up the sun, sand and hospitality!

While I was there, Graham Murray, the coach of my club Leeds Rhinos, had just been given the head coaching job at Sydney Roosters. He invited me to have a chat with them.

I was hugely impressed, both with the club's set-up and

the quality of Sydney living. Later on, in 2000, I signed with the Roosters for three years.

During that time, we had a bit of success and I absolutely loved living in Sydney and playing in the Australian NRL so, when the chance came, I didn't hesitate to sign for another three years. Once that contract was over I decided to come home, because my intention had always been to finish my career in England. Nowadays, I ply my trade with Warrington Wolves and really enjoy it.

As for Australia, I still have my place in Coogee Bay and my partner Clare, our son Leo and I have residency in the country, meaning it's always an option to go and live there permanently when the time comes to hang up my boots.

I've been to quite a few places in Australia and I think it's a magnificent place to live. For one thing, the outdoor, sporting lifestyle is great for raising kids. I would never admit any of this to my Aussie team-mates at Warrington though; you can't give an Aussie too much ammunition to use on you.

Most likely, the 2008 World Cup was my last rugby league tour down under. As a group of players, we set off to the tournament with high expectations and confidence, but didn't turn in the performances we had hoped for. And that was a huge disappointment to say the very least.

From an English point of view, this book is probably the best thing to come out of the 2008 World Cup!

ADRIAN MORLEY
JUNE 2009

INTRODUCTION

When Tony Hannan and Phil Caplan, those merry little imps from the under-world that is rugby league publishing, suggested to me that the time might be right for an Australian-based follow-up to *Up and Over*, my first thought was that it could mean rather a long walk.

That book, you might recall – and it's still available in all good book shops and a few very ordinary ones if you don't – was the chronicle of a trek on foot through the heartlands of British rugby league. It was fun to do, sold a few copies and opened a lot of doors, some of which would have been better left securely bolted. I'd had the vague idea for some time of a sequel set in the country I'd come to regard as my second home, but couldn't find the right hook to hang it on.

Then along came the 2008 Rugby League World Cup, hosted by Australia as part of the celebrations for the game's centenary there. That would involve spending several weeks in the country, some of it in places I didn't know at all well. And the brief was a flexible one. In the event of

England doing something silly like winning the thing, it would inevitably turn into a jubilant account of that unlikely event. If not, it would be more of a travel book, with rugby league always in the background and sometimes in the foreground. After two matches, I phoned Phil and Tony and said: 'Let's make it a travel book.'

Let's face it, a straight chronicle of the World Cup, from a purely English perspective, would be just too depressing – and there will have been, by this time, other people doing it better. So this book does not attempt to go down that road.

There is very little description of actual play and almost no fully-fledged interviews. Tactical analysis has been kept to the minimum; there are no maps and very few pictures. There are no diagrams and precious little practical advice on how you should live your life. Reading that wide-ranging disclaimer makes me wonder what the hell there can be left that is in it. The sad answer is that it is mainly a case of me, wandering about, looking and listening, trying to make sense of it all. There is so much I love about Australia and so much that drives me mad with bafflement – they are, not infrequently, the same things. This has been my opportunity to delve into all that, especially where I can find echoes of my beloved game of rugby league. And, believe me, when you've the best part of 300 pages to fill, you can find those echoes in the most surprising places.

It is also, in an indirect way, about places other than Australia; Papua New Guinea and New Zealand, for instance, but perhaps most of all, England. It approaches all these places with broad brush strokes and tiny sparks of insight, so apologies in advance for any sweeping generalisations that make inhabitants of any of them protest at being grotesquely misrepresented.

Thanks are due to a number of people, notably the movers and shakers at Scratching Shed, a relatively new and entirely visionary enterprise with which I am very happy to be associated. Phil and Tony I have already mentioned, but I sense that much of the hard work is done by Ros Caplan. What with this book and another of mine, *XIII Winters, XIII Worlds*, she must have transcribed close to a thousand pages of my ramblings by now. If you see a woman quietly gibbering to herself at Headingley, it is probably her.

A word of gratitude too for various travelling companions, cell-mates and flat-sharers who put up with me on the World Cup tour of duty. They included my regular valet Andy Wilson, Ian Laybourn, John Ledger, David Burke and Trevor Hunt.

If Tony Smith got it wrong with his rooming plans, some of the above cast-list probably thought at certain stages that our travel agent had been equally remiss. 'Bloody hell,' they must have thought, reaching for the earplugs, 'not Hadfield again.' Thanks too to Dave Woods, another good mate and one who fortunately had the new toy of a digital camera with him. And not to forget Ron Hill, who inadvertently provided the catchphrase for the trip, which was not something he expected to do. They were all good company and probably provided me with far more in the way of insights than they realised at the time.

The same applies to all those supporters who made the journey from the other side of the world, with most of whom I feel I must have had that awkward 'What went wrong?' conversation at some stage. Once their indignation died down, they were the epitome of long-suffering patience in heeding those wise words of advice: 'Don't let the rugby spoil the trip.' They have too much common sense to fall into that trap.

I've already admitted to not making this a book dependent on set-piece interviews, but I'm still indebted to players, coaches and administrators at the World Cup who, by and large, win or lose, remained friendly and approachable. I might spend half an hour with someone, for one phrase that sticks in the mind or takes me off in another direction, but I am grateful all the same.

I don't expect every player, particularly every England player, to agree with my version of what happened in Australia. It would take an awful lot of below-par performances, however, to dilute the respect I have for them. Having played this uniquely demanding game at a very low level for too many years, I know how much it takes to go light years beyond that standard and play it properly.

It's impossible not to admire the real warriors of the game, like Adrian Morley and Steven Price, or the game little blokes, like Billy Slater or Rob Burrow. If I sometimes seem to be having a bit of fun on their account, I hope they can all see that I'm laughing with them, not at them. This message is especially addressed to the hairy-arsed front-rowers, some of whom know where I live and one of whom has very kindly agreed to write the introduction (thanks Mozz!). There's a fair bit of piss taken between these covers, but the main victim – and rightly so, you would probably agree if you had ever seen me on tour – is myself.

Also adding to the richness of the mix that made up this book were all the meetings and ad hoc conversations I had with former players – Australian, British, Kiwi and the rest. They confirmed my suspicion that, whilst they might emerge battered and battle-scarred from a career in rugby league, they are often warmer and wiser human beings as well. One of the great pleasures and privileges of this way of life is being in their company.

It is always good as well to meet up with old colleagues from half-forgotten newspapers, who have done the sensible thing and settled on the other side of the world; people like John in Sydney and Niall in Hong Kong, who don't particularly follow the game themselves but don't mind providing a spare room or a folding bed for someone who follows it to the painful extent of watching England play New Zealand six times.

But thanks, most of all, to the good folk of Australia, especially the good rugby league folk of Australia, led out of the tunnel by people like Ian Heads, Steve Mascord and Steve Ricketts. I've been lucky with the Australian mates I've made down the years and these are three out of the top division. None of them conform to many of the Aussie stereotypes, apart from being good blokes and loving their footy. Everywhere I went, though, I benefited from one cliché about the national character that is fundamentally true. They are, for the most part, wide-open people in a wide, open country. If you can't strike up an entertaining conversation with a stranger in Australia, there is something radically wrong with you. Or you have run into Wayne Bennett on a bad day.

The last word should be for my family, who have once more endured the obsessive patterns of behaviour involved in writing a book with the stoical watchfulness of outback stockmen in the dry season. There is a new generation of grandchildren now for me to try to interest in the game: Freya, who is rather loosely allied to Salford; Marnie, who thinks the whole thing is ridiculous; and Ted who, since he turned three, has started to come into the room where we have the telly and say intensely gratifying things like: 'Grandad, can we watch the rugby?'

Yes we can, Ted, and one day, with any sort of luck at all, I'll take you to see it in a wonderful country called Australia.

DAVE HADFIELD
APRIL 2009

Stanley Gene surrounded by his wantoks

1

Townsville And The Naming Of Australia

The world is consistently unimpressed by the whole idea of a town called Townsville.

'What's the place called where you're starting this jaunt?' people ask. 'Townsville? Isn't that just like calling it town-town?'

On the face of it, there is a slight case of failure of the imagination here. A bit like places such as Wagga Wagga and Moonee Moonee – so nice they named them both twice, but not with much variety. Or the big family called the Archibalds who lived next door to my mum in her youth and who, when the twelfth son or so arrived, christened him Archibald Archibald. Or Two Bobs' mum and dad, who created the rugby league phenomenon that is Mr Robert Roberts.

One local, quoted in *Townsville: History and Mystery*, an invaluable publication obtained from the Museum of Tropical Queensland, puts it this way: 'When people ask me where I come from and I say Townsville, it sounds awful. I may as well say Hicksville and be done with it.'

It is not to be confused with Townville on the outskirts of Castleford, sandwiched between downtown Cas and the M62; it lacks that sort of glamour. Talk about giving a town a bad name.

Getting the names of things right – or, more often, wrong – has always been a central issue for Australia, even centuries before any European went anywhere near the place. Aristotle and Ptolemy called it Terra Australis Incognito – the Great Unknown Land to the South – and theorised that, although no-one had seen it, it must be there in order to balance up the earth's land masses. One thing they were sure about was that it must be connected to the South Pole, which it isn't – although on a cool day in Canberra you could be excused for thinking otherwise.

Despite this basic misunderstanding – on a par with the escaped convicts who believed that if they could get over the Blue Mountains they could make their way on foot to China – the name stuck. When Captain James Cook sailed down the east coast of Australia, that was what he called it. When he went past what is now Townsville, all the ships' compasses went haywire, due to the iron ore deposits on what was quickly dubbed Magnetical Island, now known as Magnetic Island or just Maggie. It was the start of a great Australian tradition, under which any word or name which can be shortened, must be shortened. All that time which would otherwise be squandered on those extra syllables can then be used to get a bet on or get a beer in.

Townsville – Townie to its mates – became Townsville because of a founding father who appears to have spent little more than a couple of long weekends there.

Capt. Robert Towns was a Sydney-based politician and businessman who put up the money for a port and settlement on the North Queensland coast in 1864. Although Rome wasn't built in a day, Townsville was reputedly built in eleven and consisted of 'a boiling-down works, primitive port facilities, several cottages and a couple of shanty pubs.'

Towns had high hopes that one of those establishments, The Criterion on The Strand, would become the fulcrum of civilised local society, but when the first consignment of liquor arrived on the coastal steamer, the inhabitants consumed it in three days and stayed drunk for three weeks. There are those who will tell you that Townsville hasn't changed all that much. The Cri is still there, rebuilt and painted purple, on the way to the Magnetic Island ferry and a major centre for hooning – of which much more later.

So how does somewhere like Townsville come to be the launch-pad for something like the 2008 Rugby League World Cup? Not Sydney or Brisbane, but little old Hicksville, Town-town up the coast. Well, at one stage the first game of the tournament, between England and Papua New Guinea, was supposed to be in Perth, that pristine city a million miles away on the west coast. Townsville, however, put up better financial guarantees and had the advantage of a genuine rugby league heritage. They might have clubs in the national soccer and basketball competitions, they might have Japanese links through the old cane-field workforce that made Japan resonant and well-supported visitors during the Rugby Union World Cup – henceforward to be referred to as 'that other thing' – but, first and foremost, Townsville is a league hotbed.

By the start of the First World War, just six years after the code's arrival in Australia, the Townsville Rugby League had been established as the game's first outpost in North Queensland, followed by Charters Towers, Innisfail and Cairns.

Every Lions Tour from 1928 to 1974 called there and that

perennial tourist, Ray French – still ploughing his journalistic furrow at this World Cup – recalls the squad for the 1968 tournament playing an extra game there against North Queensland. That was at the old ground near the town centre, under the shadow of Townsville's great landmark, Castle Hill, and after the game players like French, Roger Millward and Tommy Bishop ran to the top, just for the hell of it.

I can't recall any such exuberance after Great Britain's unconvincing 14-10 win in 1992 over a Queensland Residents side featuring a young forward called Steele Retchless, who was to grow to fit one of the most impressive names in the game. It was my first, brief experience of the place, and I was back three years later for the inaugural game of the North Queensland Cowboys at what was then Stockland Stadium. That whole weekend is a blur of jet-lag and ice-cold beer, because it also included the opening games at the Western Reds in Perth, the Auckland Warriors, and the South Queensland Crushers in Brisbane, as well as the first rumblings of the Super League Wars that would eventually account for two of them. The Cowboys were one of the survivors of the hostilities and, such is the see-saw nature of the National Rugby League, have since experienced both wooden spoons and a Grand Final. They should never really be short of quality players, because the area produces a disproportionate number of them. Gorden Tallis and the prolific Leeds winger, Scott Donald, are two who call Townsville home, whilst Australia's current choice of scrum-halves, Johnathan Thurston and Scott Prince, were both educated in the town.

So, when it came to doling out World Cup fixtures, Townsville's rugby league credentials were not in doubt. It had another thing going for it and that was geography. Under the tournament's bizarre format, a designated whipping-boy was needed to complete the 'super group' containing Australia, New Zealand and England. After decades of neglect, Papua New Guinea, the one country in the world where rugby league is indisputably the national sport, were rewarded by being ceremoniously presented with the short straw. You said you wanted more international competition, lads. Well, here it is.

When their justifiable indignation had died down, the Kumuls had to be given a few crumbs of comfort, in the form of venues that were reasonably handy for them. Darwin or Cairns would have been nice, if a little steamy for white fellas by that time of year and short of any big, modern stadium. Townsville, with air links to Port Moresby and an established PNG community, was a decent compromise and got the England and – most excitingly for the town – Australian gigs.

Not that it seemed, on first impressions, to be all that excited. I thought I detected a hint of a sense of occasion from the lad with purple hair manning the all-night pizza stall. 'Good job you blokes are in town,' he said.

'Oh, so you're fired up for the World Cup then.'

'No, it's just that I was bored shitless.'

As we shall see, the young people of Townsville's service industries have the happy knack of finding the right words to express the mood of the moment.

Take the pasty-faced waitress at the Greek restaurant on Palmer Street. 'Why should I be looking for a boyfriend, when the one I've got is perfect?' she asked one customer and potential suitor. It was a particularly touching tribute, as, on her previous visit to the table, she had revealed that she had just been visiting him in prison.

He's probably just a bit of a hoon. 'A who?' I hear you ask. No, a hoon. Like the Eskimo with their fifty words for snow, Australians have a whole range of carefully calibrated words for ne'er-do-wells. A typical hoon might be found doing hand-brake turns in a 'borrowed' car at four in the morning, although hooning can be a pedestrian activity as well, provided it is loud and disruptive enough. A larrikin can be equally loud and drunk, but is not necessarily bad to the core and regarded almost affectionately, whilst a lair is more of a calculating villain, who might well be adept at the great Aussie institution of the rort – the southern hemisphere's equivalent of the scam. A boofhead, on the other hand, is more of an all-purpose idiot. I came across a new category on this trip - a species of hicks-from-the-sticks yob called a bogan. These are important distinctions to be observed; call a larrikin a hoon or a hoon a bogan and he could easily take offence.

Older Townsvillites (Townsvillains? Townsvillagers?) will tell you that the main entertainment drag of Palmer Street is full to overflowing with all these groups and sub-groups. I found it rather less hoon-heavy than Bolton's Bradshawgate on a Friday night and it also has a must-see building at its far end, especially for anyone who has spent time recently following the fortunes of the Huddersfield Giants.

Midway through the 2008 season, their Australian hooker, George Gatis, announced that he was leaving early in order to go home and run the family chippy. That triggered a brief flurry of headlines along the lines of 'I've had my chips, says George' and 'We've got to get out of this plaice.'

Well, the Gatis family chippy in Townsville turns out to be a substantial seafood establishment, built on several levels and serving delicacies like scallops and lobster that are not often found on the bill of fare at The Crispy Cod on Knowsley Road. (How's that for product placement?) I wanted to see George sweating over the deep-fat fryer and ask him whether he was missing the Galpharm, but was told – and this is a phrase you will become familiar with if you last the course on this trip – that he was out of town, hunting or fishing further up the coast.

Gatis was the inadvertent cause of a little difference of interpretation that threatened to kybosh for me any friendly relations with one of the teams in the World Cup. It was all to do with Huddersfield's proud boast that they were, towards the end of the season, fielding more young, home-grown players than anyone in Super League. My response to that argument in a magazine column was a little on the churlish side. Yes, you're playing your kids, but only because your overseas players are all crocked, dropped, prematurely retired, running a chippy in Townsville or some combination of the above. What you're boasting about is picking your imports incredibly badly and now you're signing Todd Carney and Michael Korkidas. I wasn't entirely sure how their managing director, Richard Thewlis, had taken that and, as he was Scotland's team manager, it could make for an interesting exchange of views when our paths crossed later in the tournament. Eh, Jimmy?

Someone or something I already had no desire to cross paths with was Whitey the Rogue Crocodile. Rogue croc? Are there any other kind? I'm with Capt. Hook, rather than Capt. Cook, on the subject of these prehistoric left-overs; the only good croc is one safely surrounded by David Attenborough and a 20-man film crew, preferably on a different continent, or one converted into handbags and cowboy boots.

The way that Whitey became the *Townsville Bulletin*'s running front-page story throughout the build-up to the World Cup did have one beneficial side-effect, however; it made us all feel like we were somewhere wild, exotic and dangerous, which instantly whisked me back to Bradshawgate.

Down And Under

It wasn't really Whitey's fault. He was the unfortunate victim of a fundamentally misguided programme of what might be called recrocification. There he was, minding his own business on Cape York, hundreds of miles north, and hardly ever eating anybody, when he was scooped up and deposited at Barramundi Creek near Townsville, a source of 160,000 potential meals, just to see how he would get on. It's a bit like these recurring schemes to re-introduce the wolf to the Scottish Highlands. No doubt it's ecologically sound, but considerably less appealing if you have a deep-seated folk memory of your nearest and dearest being ripped limb from limb by the wee beasties.

You couldn't really call what Whitey did to the beaches of Magnetic Island a reign of terror, but it was a reign of nuisance bad enough to frighten off visitors alarmed by the sight of the ten foot croc with a Parks Department antenna protruding from his grinning head lurking offshore. Despite that homing device, attempts to catch him and ship him off somewhere quieter were unsuccessful, which kept the story going nicely.

I didn't see Whitey when I went to Magnetic Island – or Mag, as I was calling it by this stage. Part typically Australian slice of unspoilt paradise, part suburb of Townsville, Mag is an easy place to lose your bearings and worth a day out of anyone's life, although I can't guarantee that you will run into a pack of World Cup referees, well away from their usual habitat. One thing learnt from this encounter is that Australia's famous rhyming referee, Shayne Hayne, is not called Shayne at all. Apparently, his actual first name is Kevin, which raises the question of why you would change it to Shayne other than to be noticed. Which is a worry. It's like Steve Ganson changing his name by deed poll to Manson Ganson, in order to add a completely unnecessary extra layer of notoriety.

While we're at it, spare a thought for the only boy at his nursery in Brighton to rejoice in the middle moniker of Fuifui. His dad, Nigel, arrived in Townsville to the bad news that the Parramatta forward, Fuifui Moimoi, after whom he had named his son and heir, did not look as though he was going to be allowed to play in the World Cup. Seeing him play in the flesh was not the only reason Nigel had travelled half-way around the world, but it was one of them.

Tonga had tried to register Fuifui, but the problem was that he had declared his allegiance to – and played for – New Zealand the previous year. It was one of a myriad of grey areas over questions of player eligibility in a part of the world where people often quite genuinely have a foot in two or three camps, but it was the only one which ultimately went to the Supreme Court of New South Wales. In the meantime, it was disappointment for Nige, not to mention Ted Fuifui Wiskar. Mind you, his mum, Rebecca, still has a pair of fluffy slippers called after Barry Ward, the otherwise unremarkable short-haul prop who had a stint with St. Helens. From memory, the left foot is 'Barry' and the right one 'Ward.' Eccentric? Us Poms? Never.

Apart from the island previously known as M – and The Criterion, by the way, despite advertising 24-hour wet T-shirt contests, was closed on the way back - the other must-go destination from downtown Townsville is the aforementioned Castle Hill, the one run up by our energetic 1968 World Cup squad. It looms almost 1000 feet – or just over 1000 feet, if you count the cairn on top – over a generally flat landscape, so it just says: Climb me, climb me (Although preferably not after 80 minutes unarmed combat with the cane-cutters and meat-packers of North Queensland.)

I tackled Townville's loftiest peak – a description to rank alongside 'Norwich's highest mountain' – in the company of Ron Hill, a redoubtable Welsh forward who played with distinction for Castleford and Salford in the 'sixties and 'seventies. Ron would undoubtedly have been in Wales' 1975 World Cup squad, had he not been taking a year out to concentrate on his day-job. He now wears a number of rugby league hats, including that of agent to a stable of players, among them the Irish captain, Scott Grix, and briefly and bravely, Dwain Chambers; this was a long-delayed first visit to Australia.

It's always instructive to see a place through the fresh eyes of the newcomer and it was soon clear that Ron had bought heavily into the great Australian myth, for which Aussies themselves are partly responsible, that the sun always shines and that it last rained in the days of Queen Victoria. Every time a cloud drifted over, he would look reproachfully at the sky, shake his head and say: 'That's not what I was expecting.'

What neither of us was expecting as we got to the end of the grandest houses in the foothills and began the assault in earnest was a shout from a front porch. We just happened to be outside the front gate of Graham Murray, a coach whose battle honours include Illawarra, the Hunter Mariners, Leeds, the Sydney Roosters, Fiji, NSW and, most recently, the North Queensland Cowboys. Muzza offers us a lift to the top, which would just be cheating, and later becomes so concerned about our slow progress that he drives up to check on us. It's all uphill, we tell him, and that's just not what we were expecting.

Later, over jugs of iced water on the wrap-around verandah that is the essential feature of the houses they call Queenslanders, he says he has probably had enough of modern coaching and the modern rugby league player. 'They don't think they owe the game anything,' he says.

You can't accuse him of not giving the coaching caper a fair go. Among his achievements are taking the Steelers to their first final, the unloved Mariners to the final of the World Club Championship, turning Leeds into a club that could once more win things and getting the Cowboys to a Grand Final, before getting the sack a couple of years later.

He was also the coach who took Adrian Morley to the Roosters - a case of When Muzza Met Mozza – and who groomed Ian Millward for stardom, y'know what I mean? He is off to the airport shortly to collect Millward - a.k.a. Basil - but, unlike him, will not be going to the England-PNG game. In fact, he hasn't been to what is now Dairy Farmers Stadium since the Cowboys gave him the elbow and doesn't think he will.

From the top of Castle Hill, you can see the airport, the islands, the city – as it should properly be called and which it looks like from this angle – and miles inland. But from the Murrays' verandah, you get a better idea of the devastation created by Cyclone Althea in 1971, when it cut a swathe through Townsville, starting more or less in front of where their house now stands, ripping off roofs and demolishing homes. 'I bet they weren't expecting that,' says Ron.

Back at sea-level, Townsville is starting to fill up for the match. An estimated 6,500 English fans were coming to Australia for the World Cup, but only the very keenest were starting in Townsville. After all, it was a bit of a formality, wasn't it? The Kumuls were only there to get beaten by everybody, then go home and leave the big boys to get on with it. Far better, if you only had a limited time off work, to concentrate on the bigger games.

There was also a growing PNG presence in the town as kick-off grew closer, with the numbers of permanent residents swelled by the in-comers from over the Coral Sea. I like to think you can spot the new arrivals by their understandable bemusement at the trappings of modern urban life, like traffic lights. There was a wonderful TV series a couple of years ago, in which they took tribesmen from the Sepik River to London to observe their reaction. Among the sights they showed them was St. Paul's Cathedral, explaining that this was the equivalent of the spirit-house in their village and had been built by a man called Sir Christopher Wren.

The tribesmen scoffed at the ridiculousness of that. The building must have been made by gods rather than men, they insisted, but they were horrified that anyone had been allowed to put up taller structures nearby. That was an insult to the ancestors, who would be bloody furious, making it certain that everything would go pear-shaped in the village called London. I reckon they had a point.

As I got closer to The Brewery, I could hear the unmistakable sounds of a tribe marking out its territory in an alien environment – the rhythmic drumming, the demented chanting. Before I take you there, however, there is something we need to sort out and which can be put off no longer.

The Brewery is a pub; you can tell that because its main business is selling beer, some of which, like Townsville Bitter, is brewed on the premises.

Across the road is a hotel. You can tell it's a hotel because you can sleep the night there. Some pubs might be called hotels and some might have accommodation, but they're still pubs. Clear as day, isn't it? Not if you're Australian. To them, that seven star establishment on the beach in Dubai is a pub and the street-corner boozer with spit and sawdust on the walls and ceiling as well as the floor is a hotel. Is it any wonder that many of them become so confused that they never get home at all? I'm a great admirer of the wit and vigour of Australian as a living language, but this is just a case of being wrong and refusing to admit it.

And while we're at it, if Australians are so clever, how

come none of them can pronounce 'Salford' correctly. Even Australians who have coached or played for them say the A as if it's an A, whereas any scally on Langworthy Road could tell them it's a O. We could use that as a sort of modern day shibboleth, to determine who gets visas and work permits.

And the Lakes District, where on the map is that? I've heard the argument that there is more than one Lake and that the plural is therefore justified, but I think you'll find that there is only one actual LAKE – Bassenthwaite. All the rest are Waters or Meres. So we win that one as well. We might not beat you at rugby league very often, but that's another gold medal for us in the Pedantry Olympics.

It was with such thoughts running through my mind that I homed in on The Brewery, now a colourful tableau of boisterous fans in their tribal finery, enacting their primitive rituals and chanting out their incomprehensible challenges. In the interests of global rugby league solidarity, I should have gone over and greeted them in the few words I know of their native tongue, but somehow I just wasn't in the mood for Golborne Parkside and I slid swiftly past.

Strictly speaking, I should be at war with Golborne Parkside. They once staged a midnight raid on me and my *wantoks* – one-talks or speakers of the same language – at Bolton Mets and stole some players. Remarkably, their haul included a Papua New Guinean player, a loose cannon of a half-back called Jaiyoo, who claimed – spuriously, according to Stan – to be Stanley Gene's cousin. Had we been in the Highlands of PNG, it would have required a set-piece battle to sort out any rival claims to his registration. We would have put an advert in the paper and closed off the Highlands Highway for an afternoon to throw a few spears at each other. It's a little harder to arrange on the East Lancashire Road.

The late, great Peter Ward once told me that he had spent

three weeks as liaison man with the Kumul tourists in France, desperately striving to keep the news from two of the players that their villages had gone to war over some local grievance. Had they found out, they just might have felt obliged to have a go at each other. Peter succeeded in keeping the lid on it; it is not known what information, if any, about trans-Pennine hostilities reached St. Helens and Leeds players during the 2008 World Cup.

Having side-stepped the Golbornians, I found myself on the threshold of the Cowboys' Leagues Club, for a quick reminder of the importance of these institutions to life in Australia. The Cowboys' Townsville HQ is tiny by comparison with the huge clubs at Penrith or Parramatta and it has none of the classical grandeur of St George, for instance. It is on such a pifflingly small scale that it only has a few hundred poker machines – 'pokies' in case you hadn't guessed – each with its mesmerised Townsvillager pumping coins into the slot. It's as good a system of voluntary taxation as any and it kept rugby league going in Australia for years, although the imposition of tax and allowing pubs – that's pubs, not hotels – to have them has diluted their magic.

The other defining feature of Australian club-life is the ever-present dress-code. In Townsville, you could not play the pokies if you were wearing headgear, a singlet or thongs – by which they mean not the skimpy one-piece swimsuit (in which case you could see the point) but what the rest of the world calls flip-flops. I sometimes wonder at the message that is being sent out. Something like: 'By all means stuff the grocery money into the slots and leave the family without food for the week. But if you do so wearing a baseball cap, the pillars of society will crumble.'

For those who do pass muster sartorially, there are more interesting forms of gambling in the Leagues Club. In the

TAB or in-house bookies, you can place a bet on when they're going to catch Whitey.

The TAB has little doubt that England are going to beat PNG with plenty to spare, but any rugby league fan with a soul has a soft spot for the Kumuls. After all, that unique country is the one undeniable success of rugby league's declared policy of international expansion. They have Test victories over France, Great Britain and New Zealand to their credit. They have a higher level of participation in the game than any other nation. They have produced players who have appeared with distinction in the world's two fully professional competitions.

And all this has been achieved despite the most intractable problems, in a turbulent country with six hundred different languages, before you even get on to pidgin, and hardly any modern infrastructure. On a practical level, as Terry Cook notes in his book *Where Kumuls Fly* – published in Javea, Spain, of all places – Papua New Guineans are not even generally built for rugby league. Of the squad that made the first full tour of Europe in 1987, no player weighed over 14 stone and only two were over six foot. What they lack in sheer size, however, they make up for in toughness and passion. Most of all, they have achieved what they have in the game because they love it so much. Rugby league should cherish and nurture the Kumuls, but too often it has treated them like an inconvenient embarrassment. Their incorporation in the 'dead pool' with the World Cup's big three was the latest manifestation of that. What we didn't know was how they would react.

Some of the signs were good even before the tournament. They still had the talismanic Stanley Gene, plus other good Super League players in John Wilshere and Makali Aizue. And in Adrian Lam they had a coach who only needed to bring the cool cleverness he had as a player to the party to make a real difference. For an extra incentive, they had the chance to show that they could be a credible addition to the NRL, playing some of their games in Port Moresby and some in North Queensland according to what looked a very ambitious blueprint. The word was that they were setting out their stall to display their credentials in a first game they genuinely felt they could win.

And yet, lest we forget, this was an England team that looked full of promise. It was certainly not a case of leaving better players at home. Of the likely selections, only the excellent Sam Burgess – spotted strolling around Dairy Farmers with his brother, the Leeds prop, Luke, and their native guide, Scott Donald – Sean O'Loughlin and Gareth Raynor were kept out by injury. They had some good combinations taking shape, particularly between those contrasting half-backs, Leon Pryce and Rob Burrow. They had two livewire hookers in James Roby and Mickey Higham. They were strong enough in the front-row for coach Tony Smith to be able to justify leaving a fit and in-form Stuart Fielden behind.

They had had a mid-season international against France and a highly satisfactory training run against a weak Wales. They had had plenty of time to acclimatise; and, in any event, the weather in Townsville was nothing like as humid and oppressive as Ron Hill had expected. What's more, Smith had been making all the right noises about playing to our strengths and hitting the opposition out wide. All was surely set fair.

If I have one pet hate it is out-of-town grounds in the middle of nowhere. Townsville's is so far out that it is in a different town altogether – Thuringowa, an old settlement swallowed up by its hungry neighbour.

I wonder whether it is one of the towns in Australia

whose name means 'Bugger off' in some long-forgotten aboriginal language. There are quite a few of them. The first Europeans would arrive and ask the locals 'What is this place called?' They would reply along the lines of: 'Piss off, pale features, and leave us alone' and the explorers would dutifully note it down.

Talking of hunger, though, one thing you can count on in Australia, after your three-day expedition to reach the stadium, is a substantial feed. Townsville established a pattern that was to be followed, with inevitable local variations, throughout the World Cup. First the sandwiches, slightly disappointing if you thought that was all that was coming. Then the fruit, always including pineapple that tastes so fresh that it makes you suspect that not only did British shops pass off turnip in its place during the Second World War, but that many of them still do. And then – fanfare of trumpets – the pies. You have to have pies.

Those last two courses, in fact, are like a symbolic struggle for the soul of Australia. In the one hand, the wholesome and tropical; in the other, lava-hot and dribbling down your chin, a relic of the northern hemisphere and its winter comfort food that you just can't give up. The Australian badge that their players wear on their green and gold jerseys features a kangaroo and an emu holding up the shield. If you wanted to delve more deeply into a nation's divided psyche, you would be better off with a pie and a pineapple.

Between the two, the yin and yang of Aussie cuisine, our waiting-on lad is being kept pretty busy. When I mention this to him, he says: 'Yep, might have time to scratch my arse soon.' Which, a couple of centuries earlier, I might have written down as the name of the place.

All that was a mere appetiser, however, for the Asaro Mudmen. In general, I'm left cold by pre-match entertainment.

Down And Under

It's a phrase that conjures up a Tina Turner lookalike – but not very alike – tottering on an orange box at Watersheddings in 1996, on the first weekend of Super League. Or, at the other end of the scale, Diana Ross being paid a king's ransom to ride around Wembley in a limo and mime a couple of songs at the 1995 Rugby League World Cup. Give me the Mudmen any day.

They come from a village near Goroka and are noted for their short stature and for being covered in mud. It's all connected with a ruse intended to fool an enemy tribe by disguising themselves as spirits. If you drive along the right road in the Highlands, they might just nip out in front of your Jeep and, after negotiating a suitable fee, show you their best moves. You couldn't really call it dancing, more an unhurried striking of spirit poses, but it knocks spots off boy bands at Old Trafford. To be strict about it, they aren't quite the real thing – I don't think the Asaro boys do away fixtures – but it's the best Townsville's PNG cultural institute can offer. You would need to be an expert to spot the difference – that or give them a damn good scrub – and a right old stick-in-the-mud to complain.

The Mudmen had barely had time to remove their mud heads before Ade Gardner put England ahead, but three tries gave PNG a well-deserved 16-12 lead at half-time. Stanley Gene, filling the role of a play-making stand-off, was as tireless as he is timeless – and clearly the best player on the field. If the Kumuls had scored again early in the second half, they would have surely gone on to win. They had that look about them – well organised in attack and defence as well as hard-working and passionate. But the rhyming ref, Shayne's the Name Hayne, ruled that Jason Nightingale's final pass to David Moore, a hugely promising winger from the Gold Coast Titans, was fractionally forward. I've seen it dozens of times since and I'm still not convinced; one of the

English tries on the way to a 32-22 win looked a lot more dodgy.

England got away with it, but all the heroes were Papuan – especially Stanley. I will long cherish the memory of the Grand Old Man of Rugby League, iced up to his eyebrows, coming out of the dressing room for a chat, wanting not to talk about himself, but about the younger PNG players and the life-changing opportunities that could come their way after the effort they had just put in. Two members of the squad – Trevor Exton, who played that day, and Menzie Yere, who didn't – were later signed up by Sheffield Eagles, if that counts as life-changing. It certainly was for the three Fijians they signed after the 1995 tournament. Not that any of the PNG players was satisfied with a creditable defeat, mind you; the Kumuls had set out their stall to win and thought they should have won. They knew how vulnerable England were.

Before we leave Stanley's company, can we make a pact to stop calling him a liar? I've been as guilty as the next man of stories along the lines of 'How old a man is old man Stan?' for the simple reason that sports-desks like him as a subject. But he says he was born in May 1974, which makes him a perfectly feasible 21 when he played in the first of his three World Cups in 1995 and 34 now. Who are we to disbelieve him? The fact that he looks about 150 is neither here nor there. Highlanders go from beaming youth to wizened old age virtually overnight; the next time I see Jaiyoo, working at a pizza parlour the last I heard, I expect him to look like his own Grandad. And here's a shock: Stanley Gene wasn't even the oldest man in the World Cup. That honour went to that gnarled old warrior from the Wigan tribe, Mick Cassidy (born July 1973, if you take his word for it), who had just finished his last domestic season at Barrow and was enjoying one last hurrah with Ireland. Try as I might, however, I could not interest my paper, *The Independent*, in a three part series entitled 'How Old is Mick Cassidy?'

The good news for England in Townsville was limited. Lee Smith scored a hat-trick on his Test debut, the two James' – Peacock and Graham – were solid at prop and the third – Roby – typically dangerous out of dummy-half. Overall, though, the best that could be said was that it is almost compulsory for successful World Cup campaigns in any sport to begin with a below-par performance. There was that traditional first step out of the way then.

PNG were fully entitled to be the more satisfied with their display. As luck would have it, I flew from Townsville to Sydney the following morning sitting next to the chairman of their league, Albert Veratau. 'Yes, I'm proud of them, but disappointed we didn't win,' he said. 'The challenge for us now is to play as well in our next two games.'

With his eye on the bigger picture, Albert knew that the way PNG had played had already lent credibility to their ambition to play in the NRL. Before Townsville, I would have dismissed that as a pipe-dream. Now I wasn't so sure. Veratau is a realist and he knows what it will take to make it happen – starting with a decent stadium in Port Moresby and a good deal with an airline. It will also need more players who have experience at a decent level outside the country – something that is happening in a small way with that double signing by Sheffield and three more players – Charlie Wabo, Nicko Slain and Michael Mark – going to Hunslet. Brace yourselves for that cold wind that blows through the South Leeds Stadium, my friends.

Two days after leaving Townsville, I read that Whitey the controversial croc had been captured off Magnetic Island, which was good news for those who had put their money on October 28. Two days later, he was dead. The stress of the hunt was thought to be partly responsible, but not as much so as the twenty-five plastic bags plus assorted flotsam and jetsam that were found in his gut. No wonder he was a bit cranky at times.

There were some hints of foul play, as though one or more Maggie Islanders had made sure that Whitey would not return to disrupt their businesses. I prefer to view it all as a parable, in which his fate should be read as a warning to his fellow Australians about the dangers of a diet of junk food.

Ron Hill caught unawares by the unexpected appearance of Sydney Opera House

2

Sydney And The Engraving Of Australia

There were some very odd aspects to the 2008 World Cup – and I'm not just thinking of some of the very odd ways England played.

For one thing, there were three matches of various sorts before the tournament officially opened, which is a tad unconventional to say the least. For another, Sydney, long recognised as the epicentre of the rugby league universe, was relegated to what might be termed a supporting role. There were to be only two matches in downtown Sydney, with others at Penrith and Parramatta, technically part of the metropolitan area, but in fact so far out in the western sprawl that they feel like a different country entirely. Most contentious of all, the final was earmarked for Brisbane.

The feeling when that decision was made was that Queenslanders could be relied upon to turn up, even in the unlikely event of Australia not making the final. Sydneysiders have a bad reputation for clocking off as far as rugby league is concerned when the domestic season finishes and summer arrives with its counter-attractions of the beach and the cricket.

Sydney can be a bit blasé. Mind you, it has much to be blasé about. Go anywhere within sight of the harbour and you are in the most stunning cityscape anywhere in the world. It was that harbour, the best on the whole eastern seaboard and hard to match anywhere on the planet, that persuaded Capt. Arthur Phillip to establish the first European settlement here in 1788 and get the convicts busy building it. It's another place in Australia, by the way, named after someone who was never there – Thomas Townsend, Baron Sydney, the government minister responsible for the colony, although from a safe distance.

I think I was seduced by Sydney before I even set foot on the tarmac at Kingsford Smith airport for the first time almost 30 years ago, and I was hopelessly besotted by the time I unpacked my rucksack in the cheap hotel at Bondi Beach. Part of that love affair hinges on the central role rugby league plays in daily life, but if you took the game right out of the equation Sydney would still be the best city in the world. It's ravishing to look at, it's a vibrant crossroads for several continents and cultures and it's never dull or predictable.

There was a time, before the end of six o'clock closing and the arrival of influences from southern Europe and south-east Asia, when it could have been called slightly boring, but those days seem long ago. Had I been born there rather than in the North of England, or taken there at an early age, I would have been eternally grateful. As it is, I've won second prize in the raffle by making – at the last count – fifteen visits. Every time there have been new things to do, new places to see, new people – and some of the most valued same old people – to meet.

On this trip, however, following England around meant a total of just six days in Sydney, most of it occupied by something that plays only a minor role in the city's psyche – work. There was no time for any of the favourite outings: walking through the eucalyptus haze in the Blue Mountains; eating oysters by the Hawkesbury River; zig-zagging across the Pittwater on a skiff full of beer and prawns with Friendly the boat bloke. No time even for a quick visit to Woolloomooloo – the inner city suburb where surplus Scrabble letter O's go to die. It's a place immortalised in the song *The Woolloomooloo Lair* – you know the one, it's on Radio One all the time – describing the roguish practices of a nineteenth century chancer.

'The judge gives me a stare

And he says 'You are a lair'.'

Woolloomooloo and its environs are or have been home to three notable characters – the two Aussie rugby league writers best-known to English readers, Steve Mascord and Malcolm Andrews (The Strand Hotel, the pub from which he views the world, is in Woolloomooloo) plus Russell Crowe, who owns South Sydney and does a bit of acting. I don't mean to give the impression that I'm equally matey with all three; celebrity schmoozing with the Rugby League Ratpack, friend of the stars and all that crap. No, Malcolm Andrews keeps you a bit more at arm's length than that. Nor would I like to suggest which of the trio most deserves the title of The Lair from Woolloomooloo, although I reckon that what we've got here is a lair, a larrikin and a boofhead. Sort out which is which at your leisure.

I did get close to Woolloomooloo on the way to the Football Stadium, diving into the Courthouse on Taylor Square in Darlinghurst, because there wasn't quite time to get to the ground to see the first half of the curtain-raiser between an Australian Indigenous team and the Maori. As expected, it was on the big screen in the pub, much to the delight of the drinker on the next table. When Canberra's Justin Carney scored the first try of a thrilling 34-26 win for the Aborigines, my neighbour celebrated as though it was his brother who had just touched down.

'You beauty,' he whooped. 'That's my boy! Good on yer, mate!'

I was impressed. Either he was the palest Aboriginal in Australia, or this was a rare but heart-warming example of cross-cultural solidarity. The explanation was rather more mundane. 'I've backed 'em with a ten-point start,' he said.

I legged it a little quicker than usual to get to the stadium during half-time and was rewarded with a spectacular second half. It was all a bit of a consolation prize for the two teams involved, who had both wanted to be in the World Cup proper, as the Maori were in 2000. But no, the ARL were anxious to keep the 2008 tournament as compact – i.e. as cheap – as possible. Hence the mathematically insoluble problem of how to organise a ten-team competition – even though the two ethnically-based teams showed in the curtain-raiser that they could have added something.

One team nobody really envisaged being in the ten was Scotland, but they wanted it rather more than Wales did and upset the calculations in the qualifiers. Now it was possible to watch them on-screen playing France in Canberra, whilst juggling the pies and pineapples like competitors on *Crackerjack*. They lost 36-18 in a match of contentious video referee's decisions, which was enough to suggest that they were not going to be a complete embarrassment and that France might not be much cop.

Three games down and it must be time for the opening ceremony; and, sure enough, here come the swirling lights, symbolic giant rugby balls and synthesised didgeridoos – but, sadly, no Mud Men. The didgeridoo has made quite a comeback in recent years. One afternoon, I was in my favourite pub on the Rocks, The Fortune of War, when the didgeridoo busker from Circular Quay came in clad only in a loin-cloth – there's surely something in the dress code about that – for a couple of bottles of beer and nobody turned a hair. He also brought his instrument with him, which, in a pub the size and shape of the top deck of a bus, pretty much filled the place. He couldn't have just left it lying around on the Quay; for one thing, some passing female might have given it a playful blow, which is a complete no-no. No less an Australian cultural heavyweight than Nicole Kidman was warned by tribal elders that she should on no account attempt to play the didgeridoo during the pre-release publicity for the film *Australia*, as it is strictly a male-only activity. Any infraction would bring down centuries of bad luck. The newspaper headline said it all, really: Didgeridon't!

The last strains of the dirge on the didge – I'll bet you'd worked out that short version by now – had barely died away before the World Cup began in earnest with the entrance of Australia. All hail the Champions-elect! Thanks for coming, the rest of you, but you might as well go home now.

In its way, their game against New Zealand was more depressing than England versus Papua New Guinea. Australia were not, by their standards, particularly good, but they were in a different class entirely from a desperately poor Kiwi side. New Zealand were no better than on their miserable tour to England a year earlier and rather worse than in their defeat in the mid-season trans-Tasman Test. There was no sign of the improvements that were supposed to be taking place under the coaching of Stephen Kearney and his somewhat over-qualified assistant, Wayne Bennett. Australia should have scored far more than their 30 points, whilst the Kiwis, so stodgy and predictable with the ball, could have played 'til dawn without improving on the six they somehow managed to score in the first half.

Otherwise, the game was only remarkable for Johnathan Thurston opting to play, despite the killing of his uncle in a park in Brisbane the previous day. He was the victim of what is always referred to in Australia as a 'bashing' – which sounds to English ears like the sort of thing that can only happen to you in a school playground, or in the pages of *The Dandy* or *Beano*. But no, being bashed can be deadly serious, as the fate of Thurston's uncle illustrates. The two were close, so it was a big effort from him to play and play well.

If that was one story for the Monday morning sports pages, the other was the assumed demise of the World Cup. There were elements in the Sydney media who had been death-riding, if not bashing, the whole concept from the very start. Now they seemed to have all the ammunition they needed to put it out of its misery. England were rubbish. New Zealand were rubbish. All that left was a walk-over for Australia.

In a phrase that became notorious and which was used in slightly varying forms by a number of Sydney pundits, they might as well engrave Australia on the World Cup now. Contrary to popular belief, the Sydney media is not always one-eyed in support of the national team; sometimes the knee-jerk can be in the opposite direction.

I remember the late Peter Frilingos telling me after an isolated Great Britain win – it must have been '88 or '92 – that he NEVER expected to see Australia beat them again! Now, though, there was a consensus in Oz and, from what I could make out, back in England as well, that the World Cup was as good as over. I was peering warily at my computer screen for the message from my employers that said: 'Might as well come home now, don't you think?'

So you do the only sensible thing under the circumstances. Turn off your phone and head for the water, *en route* to the next match of the tournament, hoping that Tonga and Ireland might somehow revive it.

There are good ways and bad ways of getting to Parramatta, the second-oldest settlement in Australia after Sydney. Its name means either 'The place where eels lie down' or 'Get out of here, whitey, if you know what's good for you.' The bad is anything to do with road transport, because the Parramatta Road is a linear car park and recurring snarl-up on a par with the M62 on a Friday night. The best is the Rivercat from Circular Quay up the Parramatta River.

This is one of Sydney's unsung Great Ways of Getting Places, a leisurely cruise past Leichhardt – the historic home of Balmain and now the part-time base for Wests Tigers – and on past the mangrove swamps and the disused abattoirs and recycled brick-pits that became the immediate environs of the 2000 Olympics. Mercifully, there were to be no games at Stadium Australia, the main legacy left over from the games, which is fine for State of Origin and Grand Finals, but soul-destroying for any match that draws less than 50,000. It was a deeply relaxing trip and, as the sun came out properly for the first time in Sydney, Ron Hill, who had spent long hours shivering by our apartments' swimming pool, uncoiled like a buck otter in spring and declared: 'This is more like what I was expecting.'

We were not, in all honesty, expecting a great deal from the Irish, especially after rumours had come drifting down the Parramatta River that the craic had sometimes been a little too good and some players, not to mention some officials, were in holiday mode. The squad was not impressive on paper, certainly not by comparison with the side in 2000. With heavy-hitters like Terry O'Connor and

Barrie McDermott graduated to the echelons of management, they looked about National League One (or nowadays Championship) standard. They had, however, tapped into the 'brave little Oirland' sentiment in a country which, depending on how you do the maths, was colonised as much by the Irish as by the English. There has rarely been an Australian Test team without several lines of Irish descent and the fact that the Ireland squad of 2008 contained only a couple of Irish-born Irish was not a great issue. And, as if the Transportations and the Potato Famine were not bad enough, Ireland had to fly out in economy – with the chickens and goats, as their coach, Andy Kelly, put it – while the mollycoddled aristocrats representing England sipped champagne and had manicures from attentive stewardesses in business class. All grist to the mill.

On the walk from the Rivercat pier to the ground that replaced the one burnt down by over-enthusiastic Parramatta supporters when they won their first Premiership in 1981, there was a fair display of Irish or adopted Irish green, but not much belief that they could beat Tonga – even without Fuifui Moimoi, whose case was still working its way through the Australian legal system.

But the Irish, with three tries from Wakefield's Australian winger, Damien Blanch – who qualified through a granny from Belfast – went agonisingly close. It was only a couple of mistakes from the Bradford full-back, Michael Platt, that consigned them to a 22-20 defeat. Platt had been part of the Great Britain squad a year earlier and might have had a shout for an England place before Tony Smith decided he was a little too error-prone and advised him to bring his Irish qualification into play.

As it was to transpire, he was rather less error-prone than some of those considered a better bet. It was a thrilling match which did much to revive interest in the tournament, even though everyone knew that Australia's name was on the trophy.

Having seen the Irish, it was time to touch base with the Scots, which – tough job as this is – meant an expedition to Coogee. This is the beach – five down from Bondi, by my count – which has taken over since my day as the Sydney destination of choice for visiting Poms. It's a sort of Bondi for the twenty-first century, with a huge backpackers' hostel right on the sea-front, a better stretch of sand and a superior pub and café scene – provided you stay off the ice cream.

Coogee was home to that Uber-Pom, Adrian Morley, when he was with the Roosters, and he still has a unit there. A unit? I hear you cry. A unit of what?

Well, a unit of housing, I suppose, as it signifies what the rest of the world would call a flat or an apartment. I can see that calling it an apartment is out of the question – far too long – but surely flat is snappy enough. Not only has unit won the day hands-down in Australia, however, it has also crossed over into proper-job English via the medium of coach-speak.

Someone like Brian Noble might describe Lesley Vainikolo or Karl Pryce as 'a big unit.' I've just heard David Lloyd call Andrew Flintoff 'a big unit.' There is no such thing as 'a small unit' – not even if you barely come up to Rob Burrow or Alfie Langer's knee-caps. Maybe you have to follow estate agents' custom and practice and talk about compact units and bijoux units handy for all local amenities. And heaven help us if the French ever attempt a literal translation. 'That Jamal Fakir,' they might say. 'He is one spacious apartment.'

Adrian Morley was a big unit who lived in a big unit. One thing that stopped it feeling too big was a steady stream of players from Eccles and Salford Juniors dossing with him and turning out for the junior club which is, for all the worst reasons, the best-known in Australia.

But first we need to digress once more into the shadier by-ways of the Australian language. This word junior – it doesn't mean what you think it means. A junior club isn't necessarily full of kids; it just isn't a senior club – and you could play for it until you were sixty. If anyone should be familiar with this concept it is players from Mozza's old club, which is an amalgamation of Eccles with another mob, called Salford Juniors. I once played against them when their front-row must have had a combined age of one hundred and fifty and they spent the whole game attempting antique antics from the Museum of Ancient Scrummaging, like getting an arm loose, balancing on the prop's knee or blindfolding the opposing hooker. Calling them Juniors was straight out of the tradition that spawned 'Young' Mr Grace in *Are You Being Served?*

I went on the bus to Coogee, but another way of getting there is to walk along the cliffs from Bondi, past Tamarama, Bronte and Gordon's Bay, a gorgeous route further improved for a couple of weeks a year by a mind-boggling display of sculptures perched on the cliff-tops; it always seems a shame that they have to be dismantled and taken away. As you round the final headland, there is a permanent memorial to the missing players from the Coogee Dolphins – the local team that found itself caught up in the day that Australia thought would never happen.

You can feel very insulated in Australia from the upheavals in the rest of the world. It feels a long way from anywhere and it feels relatively safe, but its nearest neighbour – apart from Papua New Guinea – is Indonesia, a turbulent Muslim country with roughly twelve times its population. And, if you want to hurt Australia, you don't even have to go there; you wait until Australia comes to Indonesia and specifically to Bali.

The Coogee Dolphins were on their end-of-season trip to

Kuta Beach when the bombings there killed 202 people on 12 October 2002. That included six members of their A-Grade side, almost literally half a team. The Coogee and Randwick area suffered other casualties, among them the wife of the Australian Test prop, Craig Salvatori, but it was the loss of those half-dozen young men, celebrating the end of their season, that struck Australia and the world beyond as the most poignant symbol of the tragedy.

The club could have reacted in two ways. After such a sickening blow, their hearts could have gone out of it and the whole club could have died. Or they could do what they have done – by generating an astonishing surge of energy that has, in effect, become their memorial to their dead team-mates.

The first thing they did was to redesign their shirt to incorporate the playing numbers of the six men who died in Bali. The next was to turn themselves into ambassadors and fund-raisers on an unprecedented scale for an amateur club. The Dolphins were famous, the promoters of any out-of-town tournament wanted them and the Dolphins were only too happy to oblige. A couple of years after Bali, I travelled with them to the weekend festival that Russell Crowe organises at the Orara Valley Axemen, near one of his other homes, up in the hills above Coffs Harbour, and found them an engaging mixed bag of lairs, larrikins, boofheads and all-round good blokes. That trip made me one of the few people to actually see Crowe play rugby league – and, incidentally, he wasn't bad – but there was almost as much interest in the Dolphins as there was in his collection of ex-pro heavies like Gorden Tallis, Mark Carroll and Mark Geyer. This celebrity victim status doesn't sit well with everyone. 'You're only here because of those blokes who died,' one warm-hearted current Test player once told them.

There are also those in the South Sydney Juniors

competition, in which Coogee play, who are mean-spirited enough to resent their fame. Certainly anyone who comes to the area from out of town, out of state or out of Salford is likely to have heard of them and quite fancy playing for them.

The result is that the Dolphins have never been better off for players and have won a couple of Grand Finals. They have become something they aspired to be – a successful rugby league club – and something they can never have imagined, by also becoming a famous one. They have raised over $1 million for various charities and like to think they have done the right thing by their mates, which is what matters in the end. A few days after this, the Indonesians took three convicted bombers to a clearing near their prison on the outskirts of Djakarta and executed them by firing squad, which once more required the bereaved of Coogee to be interviewed for their reaction. Some of them, at least, felt as though a line had been drawn under the episode.

The Dolphins are based at the Coogee Palace Hotel – a pub, naturally – at one end of the beach. Up at the other end are Scotland, licking their wounds after France and preparing to play Fiji.

The good news is that Richard Thewlis is prepared to concede that Huddersfield's overseas recruitment is a legitimate source of mirth. He concedes it through clenched teeth, but he concedes it. No problems there then, although a Highland dirk did whistle past my ear later that day. Thewlis is more concerned with the circumstances of Scotland's defeat by France, which he puts down to a combination of poor decisions from the officials and below-par play from his own team. It was one of the more impressive aspects of this World Cup – the way that the minnows were not satisfied with honourable failure.

There was a homely family atmosphere in the Scots'

hotel, with their captain, Danny Brough, strolling through reception with his little lad perched on his shoulders. Had he not opted to be Scottish, he might have had a shout as second-choice scrum-half for England, certainly on his early-season form.

The first family of Scottish rugby league was not in evidence, though, contrary to what The Beatles sang, with rare prescience, on an obscure album called *Sgt. Pepper*, when they promised that 'the Hendersons will all be there.' The Henderson bothers – Ian, Andrew and Kevin – had all been given time off to go up the coast to see their dad, Martin, who was recovering from a major operation. They are a classic case study into what makes international rugby league so confusing. Born in Torquay, brought up in Australia and attached at various times to clubs in England, Australia and New Zealand, they have the potential to qualify for half the teams in the World Cup, but chose to use their dad's Scottish birthright to play their hearts out for them. They had just become the first trio of siblings to play side-by-side in a World Cup match, beating Tonga's Paea brothers – all born in Sydney – by a few days.

Ian, formerly of Bradford and now of the New Zealand Warriors, had better tread a little warily next time he comes to England. In an Australian interview, he was asked about the worst place he had ever lived and opted unhesitatingly for Castleford, where he once shared a house with Andrew, describing the town as full of obese drunks with rotting teeth. It was a sort of Leon Pryce, Blackpool is better than Bondi, in reverse and the best advice I can give him, should he ever return to Cas, is to claim that he was misquoted and was really talking about Featherstone.

Whilst with the Hendersons, let's get this thorny question of who qualifies for whom out of the way once and for all. I can do no better than refer you to the crystalline clarity of the RL International Federation's own words on the subject. Pay attention, because there will be a test towards the end of the book.

'1. A player is eligible to play an International Match for:
The country in which he was born;
The country in which either of his parents or any of his grandparents were born;
The country which has been his principal place of residence for a period of three years up to the date of his selection;
The country for which he last played representative International Rugby League football at any age level prior to the introduction of this Constitution;
A country for which he has gained Senior International honours in any sport.

'......3. A player who is eligible for more than one country shall be entitled to elect for which country he wishes to play. When a player plays a Senior International Match for a country, he is deemed to have elected to play for that country. Subject to Rule 3.5, once an election is made the player may not play Senior representative rugby league for any other country until the end of the next World Cup tournament, or the expiry of two years, whichever is earlier ('Election Period').

4. After the expiry of an Election Period, the player may elect to play for another country, if he is eligible, but once he so elects (or is deemed to elect by playing in a Senior International Match) he may not play for

another country until the expiry of another
Election Period.

5. During an Election Period, a player may
change from one country to another for which
he is eligible, pursuant to Rule 3.1, with the
approval of the Federation (but he may only
change once in each Election Period).'

I'm glad we've got that cleared up. Obviously, those are only edited highlights, but enough, I confidently expect, to explain everything, even the cause célèbre of Fuifui Moimoi.

In fact, the whole issue of international qualification is a horse that has long since bolted, not just from our stables, but from those of every other sport as well. It's never going to look right that Henry Paul or Brad Thorn can play two different sports for two different countries, but the rah-rahs didn't worry about it unduly during that other thing of theirs, so perhaps we should stop beating ourselves up about it. There were those who suffered agonies over England having an Australian-born coach and an 'impact' forward from Samoa, but Tony Smith and Maurie Fa'asavalu could have been little green men from the planet Zog for all I cared, if they had done the business.

If you wanted to go the whole hog, you could just stop policing the issue by letting people play for anyone they fancied. If Mick Cassidy, for instance, wanted to be a Papua New Guinean for a while – and God knows he looks old enough – who are we to stand in his way?

One Scot about whose credentials there could be no qualms was Paddy Coupar. A 22-year-old student, he was born in Blairgowrie – yes, Blairgowrie in Scotland – and played for Edinburgh Eagles, which made him the only player selected from the Scottish domestic competition. It wasn't supposed to be like this. The original aspiration was that each competing nation should have at least half a dozen home-based players in their squad. That was a worthy ambition, but anyone who has seen the local comps in Scotland and Ireland knows that there are precious few players there, at this early stage of development, who you could put on the field against battle-hardened veterans of the NRL. Someone could get seriously hurt. There was some hurried lobbying, not just from the Celtic fringe but also from the South Pacific, and the requirement was quietly dropped. The Scots brought only Coupar, whilst Ireland brought three products of their domestic game – including Wayne Kerr, a player whose name, for some unknown reason, created hilarity whenever it was mentioned. Someone suggested writing a celebration of rugby league in Ireland, entitled *XIII Wayne Kerrs*, but so far I have resisted the temptation.

Anyway, Paddy Coupar proved to be an ambitious and articulate young man, albeit one somewhat stunned by the experience of rubbing shoulders with some of the world's best players. Apart from the full-time professionals in the Scots squad, the hotel in Coogee was the base for Australia for part of the tournament; so over there, you might have Lockyer and Thurston and over there, Paddy Coupar.

Thrilled as he was to get the time of day from players like that, it was the slightly less celebrated names in the Scottish squad from whom Coupar felt he was learning the most.

'Everyone has so much more experience than me,' he said. 'People like Danny Brough are giving me so much knowledge and information. I see it as part of my role to take it back to Scotland to help improve the level we play at there.'

The Scots players also looked after Paddy when he got a run off the bench against Tonga in the ranking match. Their coach, Steve McCormack, had used him very carefully, but he *had* eventually used him, having judged from his attitude in training that he was capable of a brief outing.

As for the advice from the more senior members of the squad, it is to be hoped that it included giving the mixed sorbet a swerve in the hotel – pub – next door.

The presence of the Scots – and even the Australians – was not the biggest news in Coogee. The front-page headlines were reserved for a far more distasteful matter. On October 5, a customer named Jessica Whyte ordered the frozen delicacy in the Coogee Bay Hotel after she and her family had asked the staff to turn the music down. She realised that something was badly wrong and spat it out, to find that it contained what appeared to be a deposit of human faeces. That was the start of a stink that raged in the Sydney dailies for weeks, although eventually Mrs Whyte and the hotel reached a settlement – reported to be $20,000 - in compensation for the bad taste left in the mouth.

It was the second major blow in a couple of years for the Coogee Bay, following the loss of the lucrative Adrian Morley Guinness contract when he returned to England. I confidently expect them to bounce back, however. The good people of Coogee are too resilient to make a crisis out of a drama. And somewhere in a back room, some enterprising bookie will be taking bets on the next flavour of ice cream to be implicated in a similar scandal anywhere in Sydney. My money is on Chocolate Chip, with Rum and Raisin as an outsider coming up on the rails.

Waiting by the Yarra for the word of coach Smith

3

Melbourne And The Bushranging Of Australia

Much as it pains me to have to admit this, but if you want to witness the Australian sports fan at his most fanatical you have to turn your back on Sydney, Brisbane and the rugby league hotbeds of the east coast and look instead to Melbourne.

It has Australia's biggest horse-race, its biggest cricket crowds – the sheer scale of the Melbourne Cricket Ground makes the Sydney Cricket Ground feel like the Lancashire League - the Australian Open Tennis, plus probably its best-supported domino championship and definitely its best-supported club football competition. I'd only been there twice before, quite briefly and in unbroken rain. Manchester, I'd thought, but on a really bad day. I had a pretty low opinion of the place, but I still had to admit that it was the sporting capital of Australia.

That is all the more remarkable when you consider that it has been achieved despite the handicap of a code of football that is incomprehensible to most of the rest of the world. The game they flock to in Melbourne is Australian Rules Football - okay, let's get busy cutting that down to size – Aussie Rules, just plain Rules, even plainer football, or at its most minimal, footy.

Football in Melbourne means this strange affair of sleeveless shirts, high catches, monster kicks into the crowd past men in white coats and hats who look like ice-cream salesman and massive crowds, rugged-up against the cold of the Victorian winter, who appear to understand what's going on.

For all its 'game of the people' image of itself, Aussie Rules started life in the same way as most codes of football – with the notable exception of rugby league. A gang of ex-public schoolboys got together and drew up a set of rules. For the game that was to become Melbourne's obsession, they drew upon a variety of sources. There were various football formats which were in operation in England in the mid-nineteenth century, especially Sheffield Rules – which was notable for having no offside and probably lies at the root of the way the game can sometimes look like Aussie No-Rules. There was a distinct influence from Gaelic Football, although academics have argued ever since over how direct and pervasive that influence was. There was also a nod towards an Aboriginal ball-game called Marn Grook and, just for good measure, they decided it should be played on cricket ovals. No wonder they finished up with such a dog's breakfast.

As a game to keep you fit during the winter off-season from cricket, it is hard to fault Rules, because you have to run around like a lunatic to cover the broad acres of a cricket oval, especially one like the MCG. The mystery to non-Melburnians is why anyone should want to watch you doing it. It has its spectacular moments and its high marks are as good a way as any of training prospective rugby league full-backs – which it is what it sometimes turns out to be doing in the border areas between the two codes. The most annoying thing about it is a quite undeserved reputation for toughness, where the reality is that there is no actual tackling as we would understand it and the worst that can happen to you is the occasional glancing blow from a low-flying sleeveless beanpole on his way back to earth.

Mind you, Melburnians love it. They stick to it through thick and thin, turning a deaf ear to the global siren-song of round-ball football – which you have to admire. It is also undeniable that footy in Melbourne out-draws league in Sydney by a wide margin, something Rules fans love pointing out. The average crowd for their regular season matches in the AFL in 2008 was very nearly 37,000, with an aggregate of over 6.5 million. Compare that with the NRL, which managed a paltry 15,591 and a total of under 3 million. No contest.

Sydney's best defence is that there is a lot more to do there. It has a hundred beaches, from Palm Beach at the north end of Manly Peninsula to Cronulla in the south; Melbourne has St. Kilda. If everyone who is out on the water on any given weekend was rounded up and dragged to the rugby league, the figures would look a lot closer. The fact remains, though, that, as a very broad generalisation, Sydney is a place for doing things and Melbourne a place for watching them.

There is another sense in which this comparison is not taking place on a level playing field. The slightly sniffy sections of Sydney society who turn up their noses at something as identifiably local and blue-collar as rugby league on principle will watch an imported game like Rules because it is innocent of the same class connotations. The same process does not seem to work in reverse in

Melbourne, where the Storm struggle along on 12,000 despite their considerable success. That success, since their foundation in 1998, includes winning two Grand Finals and nurturing some young talent as good as any the game has ever seen. In the squad for the game against England, for instance, they had the youngest-ever Australian centre partnership in Greg Inglis and Israel Folau, a freak of a full-back in Billy Slater and one of the modern game's outstanding hookers in Cameron Smith.

The down-side is that Melbourne has yet to produce a home-grown player of any note. All those four are Queenslanders, making in reverse the diagonal journey, missing out New South Wales, that so many Victorians make for their holidays. It is upon their feeder network in Brisbane that the Storm's achievements have been built. That and their mastery of what many find the most infuriating aspect of the contemporary game – the battle for supremacy on the floor. No-one is better at the wrestling techniques that amount now almost to a game within a game. It's not pretty, but it is highly effective – and they do have the considerable redeeming feature of spectacular backs like Inglis and Slater. They do not yet, though, have the sporting public of Melbourne locked in a grapple tackle.

Taking the whole nation into account, the AFL's expansion policy has been far more successful than rugby league's. Since the early 'eighties, what was the Victorian Football League has added clubs in South and Western Australia, both of which were already Rules strongholds, and in Sydney and Brisbane, which were not. They have not been guilty of setting up shop in cities and then pulling out as part of a political fix, as league did in Perth and Adelaide.

What Rules lacks, even by comparison with rugby league, is a credible international dimension. The AFL's website refers to competitions running in places like

Denmark and Germany and there is a development officer working in schools in Indonesia, but it is all on an almost invisible scale. There were a few one-sided scorelines in the Rugby League World Cup and some hundred-point romps in that other affair with the two extra players on each side a few years ago, but they would be nail-biters compared to Australia against anyone at Rules. There was a tournament for other countries in Melbourne in September, with Papua New Guinea beating New Zealand in the final, but it passed off virtually unnoticed.

The same cannot be said of the visit of the Irish. Whatever the precise nature of their historic connection, Gaelic Football is Rules' only living relative and the two have been estranged for many generations. Since 1998, however, they have been getting together for family reunions which have been appropriately volatile.

The 2007 series was scrapped completely because of violence on and off the pitch the previous year and welding two different games together is always problematic. Under what the AFL calls International Rules and the Irish call Compromise Rules – they can't even agree on that – you have the round ball and goal-nets of the Gaelic game and mostly the Australian custom and practice elsewhere on the pitch. It is worse than a dog's breakfast; it's a dog's breakfast designed by committee, but in 2008 it was back on the menu and booked in at the MCG two nights before the Australia-England World Cup game up road at the Telstra Dome. That ensured that, apart from thousands of still hopeful Poms, Melbourne was full of freckly-faced, red-haired, horribly sunburnt Irish, finding their way to back-street bars that sold Guinness.

I would have joined them at the MCG out of pure curiosity, but for another event taking priority. Remarkably, the part-timers – the Gaelic Athletic Association still being amateur and quite aggressively so – beat the highly paid professionals by four points, in front of 42,000 punters. Having won by a single point at Perth a week earlier, that made the Irish unlikely International Rules Champions, exposing the Aussie Rules blokes to the jibe that they were the only people in the world playing their weird game to any standard and they still managed to finish second.

By this time, I was warming to Melbourne. The key to that is that you just haven't got to expect it to be Sydney. It is a city that has evolved from its European roots, rather than exploded. It still looks north for its inspiration, rather than across the Pacific towards California. Which means that a lot more of its old buildings have survived than have in Sydney, which in turn means that it has better pubs. Not that pubs really entered into the equation at the end of my first full day there, not with a Victorian Microbrewery Showcase just outside Flinders Street Station. Not a beer festival, you understand; I don't like beer festivals – your feet stick to the floor – and I wouldn't have gone. But a Microbrewery Showcase is a different matter. It would have been positively rude to have ignored that – and BBC Radio Manchester's indefatigable Trevor Hunt thought so as well. (Indefatigable? It means you never get tired, Trev.)

We were rewarded with the sight of hundreds of Melburnians getting it down their necks on their way home from work. You paid your money and got a sheet of twenty-seven tokens, each one exchangeable for a sample of a different beer. Only a small glass, but twenty-seven of them add up. They add up to twenty-seven, in fact, or they do at the start of the evening. The message on the array of tokens was a welcome one. Drink responsibly, it read. Only in Australia....

While we're all pissed together, this might be as good a time as any for a brief digression on the subject of Australian beer measures. When I first lived in Sydney, there was only one pub in the city that served pints and people would come from miles around, just to see these gargantuan buckets of beer that had to be lifted from table to mouth with the aid of a block and tackle. Elsewhere, it was all middies and schooners. But beware, you can drink fifty middies (around half a pint apiece) and still be considered a sober, upstanding member of society; sup one schooner (about three-quarters of a pint) and you're a dribbling piss-pot. Other states had different measures and names, with the rule of thumb that, as you went further north, you drank smaller glasses – but more of them – in order to avoid the ultimate horror of your beer becoming 'hot' – that is, not completely frozen - before you can drink it.

The big surprise since then has been the role Australia has played in the world-wide fight-back of the pint. For a country that meekly gave up its ton and its mile, its pound sterling and its pound weight, it has done a manful job of putting all hands to the pumps in defence of the 20 oz glass, which has even come under pressure in Britain. Pints are widespread in pubs and clubs now, but, mysteriously, do not carry the same stigma as schooners. Even more mysteriously, when I start to go native after a couple of weeks in Australia, a pint starts to seem a bit too much – a thing I never thought I would say. A middy is not enough – it never was. But, as in the story of Goldilocks and the Three Beers, a schooner is just about right.

It was important to get these matters clear before one of the most important pub nights of the whole trip. In an ideal world, I would have much preferred to be at Penrith to see Tonga versus Samoa live, but the itinerary just didn't work out that way. The alternative was to find a bar, preferably one with a Tongan/Samoan clientele, and watch it there. The Turf, just down the street from our apartments, seemed as though it would be perfect. They have the whole business of watching sport sorted out there – but, hey, this is Melbourne. They have a timetable decreeing what each of their numerous screens will be showing at any given time and even with the Aussie-Ireland schmozzle on the biggest of the plasma jobs, the back room was set aside for the South Pacific hostilities.

Everything continued to go smoothly when I found a group of unmistakably Polynesian appearance clustered around the designated TV on the night. It meant the inevitable question: 'Who you supporting, bro'?' – an important one to answer correctly, relations between Tongans and Samoans being the volatile proposition that they are.

'Ur, you know, as long as rugby league's the winner. What about you blokes?'

'Us? We're half and half.' By which he meant not that they were six of one and half a dozen of the other, but that each of them was part Tongan and part Samoan. When Tonga scored, they were Tongan and they got the beers in – pints, naturally. When Samoa scored, their Samoan heritage reasserted itself and they got the beers in. They were also probably New Zealanders and Australians, but only during the half-time interval. It was like a little seminar on the complexities of nationality in the South Pacific.

It was the Samoan side of my new best mates' psyche that went home satisfied. A team that looked suspiciously like a Kiwi Veterans XIII was a little too good for Tonga in a 20-12 win and it was a memorable experience watching one of my favourite players, David Solomona, slipping impossible passes out of the tackle with my chums from the islands. It wasn't quite the World War III that had been predicted, but it was a stirring, intense contest which did more than its share to re-establish the World Cup as something worth watching.

The following evening was more problematic. The Turf had foolishly gone overboard on the Bledisloe Cup – too many players running around a field in Hong Kong – and it was decreed that every screen in the joint would be switched over to that, even before the end of our France-Fiji game, not to mention New Zealand against PNG straight after it. Negotiations were opened with the Irish Times bar around the corner. If they would nail their channel selector onto the rugby league for the night, we could promise them that they would sell an extra pint or two.

We delivered on our side of the bargain, rather more than France did on theirs, because – apart from the obvious – they turned out to be the biggest disappointments of the whole World Cup. This was supposed to be the tournament when they showed the benefits of the Catalans Dragons playing with such success in Super League. Instead, it looked as though the main effect of Super League had been to leave them completely knackered. Their general lack of direction was a reminder that a number of the Catalans' key positions are occupied by Australians – not that this is unique to them. With hindsight, it also looks obvious that relying on one month a year with a flown-in coach, even one as experienced as John Monie, was a recipe for under-achievement.

Whatever the combination of reasons, France were played off the park in Wollongong by a Fijian side who were an immediate gust of fresh air through the World Cup. Jarryd Hayne (no rhyme, no relation) showed all the talent he had been threatening to squander in the NRL, whilst Akuila Ueta looked a dazzling prospect on the wing with his three tries in a 42-6 victory.

Apart from a war-dance that was a little less heavy on confrontational theatrics than Tonga and Samoa the previous night, the Fijians were notable for singing hymns before, after and, I think at one stage, during the game. The Pacific Islands do seem to be a very devout part of the world; if there is an agnostic player from that neck of the woods, let alone an honest atheist, we have yet to hear from him.

In the other game, PNG, much as they themselves had feared, suffered a big emotional let-down after their efforts against England, losing 48-6 to New Zealand on the Gold Coast.

It's strange how the word gets around, because by the time of the second game there was a veritable Who's That of rugby league in the Irish Times. That included one of the game's more interesting characters, Graeme Bradley, the former Bradford stand-off. I reckon The Penguin, as he's known, must have been one of the most horrible players of modern times to play against; every snide trick in the book and a frame like a bag of chisels when you tackled him. It's almost conventional to surmise that, the more rugged the player on the pitch, the cuddlier off it. Not true of Bradley, folks, he's a bit of a bag of chisels in real life as well.

I remember him once abducting me and my taxi driver as I arrived at my hotel in Edinburgh for a quiet, early night. He needed a cab and I had one, so I was fare game. He was in town on a double sporting mission, the Melbourne Cup – The Race that Stops Australia – on the Tuesday and, before that, Australia against England; apart from anything else he is a big mate of Tony Smith. The Penguin had a theory. It would be a thoroughly good idea to lose heavily in Melbourne and then come back to beat an under-done and complacent Australia in the final. 'You mark my words,' he said. 'That's what's going to happen.'

There wasn't long to wait to find out whether England were going to fit in with the first part of that philosophy, but I had things to do first. I'd come to the reluctant conclusion that not only was Melbourne the centre of gravity of Australian sport, it was also the place you had to look for the key to Aussie iconography, to what it is that makes an Australian folk-hero. Within a few hundred yards in Melbourne, you can breathe in the presence of two whose names have entered the language.

It doesn't fit in with our new image as a band of hard-boiled journalistic hatchet-men, just waiting and longing for the national team to fail, so that we can swoop like vultures and dine off the corpse, but some of us get pathetic big-match nerves. I'm probably the worst; I need plenty to do or I'm just a menace to myself and everyone else.

Thus it is that by mid-morning on match-day I'm tucking into some early antipasti at an Italian pavement café on Lygon Street, as forty or fifty restaurants fill up with families doing the same. It's a fine example of the European-but-better trick that Melbourne pulls off so successfully, that blend of old-world style and Australian abundance, and it sets a person up handsomely for a rigorous day's research.

In Melbourne Cup week, it seemed only fitting to pay one's respects to the nation's great equine icon. As usual in this part of the world, however, definitions are not quite straight-forward, because Phar Lap was foaled in New Zealand in 1926.

Like Russell Crowe, Willie Mason and most of Crowded House, the chestnut gelding was assimilated by the bigger place across the Tasman and became a symbol of Australian resilience during the early years of the Great Depression. His finest hour was winning the Melbourne Cup in 1930 in the proverbial canter, after which he was shipped off to the Americas to show the Yanks a clean pair of heels. It is here that the story of Phar Lap – the name means 'sky flash' or lightning in Siamese, or what we would now call Thai – takes on its mythic dimension. After winning his first race in Mexico, the horse was found in severe pain and haemorrhaged to death within hours. There has been debate and conflicting medical evidence ever since over whether Phar Lap died of natural causes or of a massive dose of arsenic administered to him by vested interests who feared that he was just too good. Needless to say, Phar Lap has become legendary as the brave Aussie battler, done down by the outside world, and, stuffed and mounted, he is by several lengths the most popular exhibit at the Melbourne Museum.

Strictly speaking, Phar Lap is not quite all there – and I'm not just thinking of the bits they took away when they made him a gelding. New Zealand's claim to him is recognised by his skeleton residing in Wellington, whilst Canberra is home to his remarkable heart. Remarkable because, at over 13lb, it is almost twice the size of the average horse's.

They have a replica of this exceptional organ in Melbourne and schoolchildren are encouraged to sweat and strain to lift it from its table. It has entered the Australian lexicon; there is no higher compliment than being described as having 'a heart like Phar Lap.'

There is plenty more to engage the interest at the Melbourne Museum, including the dodgy schoolboy outfit worn by Angus Young of that other Australian institution, AC/DC. Judging by its minuscule size, though, it looks more of a fit for Wee Janette Krankie or Jimmy Clitheroe. For the ultimate Australian folk-hero and fashion icon, you have to look elsewhere.

Melbourne Gaol closed in 1929, but since 1972 it has been open to visitors – and a gloomy old joint it is too. Most of Victoria's notable villains did time within its walls during its working life and one hundred and thirty-six of them were executed there. The most celebrated, by far, was Ned Kelly, hanged in 1880, at the age of just 26. For reasons that are rather difficult to pin down precisely, his name has resonated through Australian life ever since.

His father, Red Kelly, was an Irish convict shipped out to

Van Diemen's Land – now Tasmania – for, the most popular version has it, stealing pigs. On his release, he settled in Victoria, married and raised a large family. Edward – known from the start as Ned – was always something of a problem child. His first arrest continued the family's troubles with pork, when he was charged with assaulting a Chinese pig-farmer, the unforgettably named Ah Fook. He was later jailed for sending a woman a letter containing a pair of calf's testicles.

His path towards criminal immortality did not have a glamorous beginning. Nor are the circumstances which led to him and his gang going on the run entirely clear. Ned had undoubtedly been dabbling in horse stealing and cattle rustling. A police constable named Fitzpatrick came to investigate and later claimed to have been attacked by him and his brother, Dan. They denied even being there, but, not expecting to be believed, headed for the bush with two of their mates. That made them bushrangers, with Ned destined to become by far the most famous of that breed, despite the brevity of his career.

At Stringybark Creek, there was a shoot-out that left three policemen dead – two of them from shots from Ned - and the Kelly Gang were now Victoria's Most Wanted. Their legend grew with bank raids in the small country towns of Euroa and Jerilderie, both carried out with more ingenuity than the average bushranger could manage, including impersonating the police and claiming to be on the trail of 'the notorious Ned Kelly.' The second of the bank-jobs also produced the Jerilderie Letter, an eight-thousand-word self-justification in which Ned complained of the treatment of Irish Catholics by the English and Protestant settlers. Another detail which has helped stoke a Robin Hood image is that, as well as getting away with the then huge sum of £2000, he also burnt all the townspeople's mortgage deeds.

Down And Under

It is the nature of his demise that is the true stuff of legend. Holed up with seventy hostages at the pub in Glenrowan, around one hundred and sixty miles north of Melbourne, the Kelly Gang not only came out shooting, they came out clad in the home-made armour, with helmets like upturned buckets, that has been such a powerful Australian image ever since. The armour worked, up to a point. The police bullets that hit it bounced off harmlessly, but unfortunately the gang had no armour on their legs. Ned was wounded repeatedly and captured, still wearing a green sash given him by the father of a boy he once saved from drowning; the other three members of his gang died.

In Melbourne, he was found guilty of one of the murders at Stringybark Creek and sentenced to hang. He told the judge that he would be seeing him soon and, sure enough, Sir Redmond Barry died twelve days after Kelly's hanging, from the effects of a carbuncle on his neck. The execution had gone ahead despite a petition of an estimated thirty thousand signatures pleading for clemency and a demonstration outside the gaol on the appointed day. Contemporary accounts noted that the majority of the crowd consisted of youths 'of a larrikin appearance.' Australia's larrikin tendency had found its patron saint and martyr. Under the circumstances, it was a shame that he could not come up with better last words than 'Such is life' or a mumble which might have been: 'It has come to this.' He would have been better recalling his early escapades with an 'Ah Fook' or 'Calf's Bollocks,' but he was not a master of the one-liner.

He was to prove indelibly memorable, however. The story of the Kelly Gang, or variations upon it, has become a staple of Australian literature, song, film and television. There is no accolade, except perhaps having a heart as big as Phar Lap, to match that of being 'as game as Ned Kelly.'

Maybe that is what accounts for his weird little legacy to

rugby league. Needless to say, there is no direct connection; indeed, during his lifetime, he would have regarded NSW and Queensland as a foreign country. But there is something about the image of the rebel and renegade, the man who keeps coming at you, even with holes shot in his legs, that chimes with the game.

If your surname is Kelly, there is an even-money chance that you will be known as Ned. The Irish coach, Andy, isn't; his brother, the former Welsh boss, Neil, often is. One of Australia's greatest-ever front-rowers, Noel Kelly, always has been; he even introduces himself as Ned. If you look a bit of a bushranger, all the better. There were some beauties in the 1980s: the Cleal brothers, Noel and Les; Geoff Robinson, who had a season or two marauding for Halifax; Kerry Helmsley, who played for Wigan in the 1984 Challenge Cup final; Gary Hambly, who had the best beard of the lot and used to go off on single-handed expeditions during the close season. Melbourne Storm have had a classic in recent times in the splendidly hirsute Kirk Reynoldson.

When any of the above have a half-way decent game, it has been compulsory to throw in a 'Ned Kelly lookalike' line among the bushranger references. We are the willing inheritors of the Ned Kelly Myth. We like the outlaw image; even Billy Slater, who to the best of my knowledge has never so much as held up a stagecoach, is Billy the Kid.

At Melbourne Gaol, you can see Ned Kelly's death mask and buy scale models of his armour. In the gift shop, there are sets of little helmets that you could arrange across your chimney breast, like the pot ducks in Stan and Hilda Ogden's living room in *Coronation Street*. You can even inspect the gallows, although rather than the originals, they are a recreation for one of the numerous films about the life of this most famous of all Australians – although Don Bradman would run him close. So I might not have seen the gallows where they hanged Ned Kelly, but I have certainly seen where they strung up Mick Jagger, which is what most critics would agree he deserved for his performance in the title role.

The most poignant story about Melbourne's gallows concerns neither of them, but a master carpenter who was once incarcerated there. He was given the job of dismantling the deadly contraption and putting it together again at the more modern Pentridge Prison. Having done that, he became one of its first victims, as he had been awaiting a death sentence. It was with that rollicking yarn in mind that I went off to see England play Australia.

It had been a rather odd build-up to the match. I should have sensed that something strange was going on at the first England press conference at Olympic Park on the banks of the Yarra River. Having asked a few innocuous questions, we had to go and hang around the riverbank like some lost indigenous tribe, pretending to have gone away, until the dreaded Australian media departed. At that point, we could sidle back surreptitiously to be told nothing else of value. Before all that, there was at least the chance to have a chat with Garry Schofield, which was as good a way as any of reliving British rugby league's finest hour in Melbourne.

It was in 1992 that the ARL took an Ashes Test away from Sydney and Brisbane for the first time to Princes Park in the suburb of Carlton. It was not an experiment they had repeated over the next sixteen years, because our brave boys kicked ass that day. They won so comfortably – 33-10 after leading 23-0 early in the second-half – that, unlike any other knuckle-gnawing victories in living memory, you could sit back and relax with a big brandy and an even bigger cigar. I did so in distinguished company in an overspill media box, where my neighbours – hold onto that word – included Roy Masters, Warren Ryan and the actor who played Jim in the premier Aussie soap. 'Struth,' says Jim. 'You wouldn't believe this script' – which, coming from somebody who had come back from the dead three times, is what they would call on Ramsey Street 'a big statement.' A reminder, too, that on top of everything else, Melbourne can claim to be at the heart of Australian popular culture. Apart from *Neighbours*, it is home to Dame Edna and the criminally under-rated Bushwackers, who sing the definitive version of *The Lair from Woolloomooloo*.

It wasn't a bad Australian side that day, either; Mal Meninga, Laurie Daley, Allan Langer – bit-part players like that – but a Great Britain side captained by Schoey and including an all-Wigan pack was just far too good.

After a sixteen-year gap, rugby league doesn't need two Garry Schofields, but it probably does need one. The game's favourite Jeremiah, to invoke the Old Testament's most pessimistic prophet, is not everybody's cup of tea. Indeed, he can come across like a more embittered version of Private Fraser in *Dads' Army* – 'Doomed....We're all Doomed.' When current players and coaches complain about negative comment from old-timers, they usually mean that Schoey has been at it again. The trouble is that, unlike Nostradamus, he's usually right.

So asking him whether he senses a repeat of 1992 in the air invites only one obvious answer. No, he does not. Not a chance. We don't have the quality. It must be an uplifting experience, being on one of Garry's supporters' tours – The Doom and Gloom Special.

It just so happens that those three Aussie easy-beats I mentioned a little earlier were all there that week to help celebrate Melbourne's other big rugby league events. In 1994, they staged the second State of Origin match of the series at the MCG, in front of a then record crowd for a game in Australia of 87,161. New South Wales, captained by Daley, beat Queensland, with Meninga and Langer, 14-0. In 2009, the first Origin match was scheduled for the Telstra Dome and all three were there, in their various capacities, for the launch of that once unimaginable concept; Meninga as Queensland coach, Alfie as assistant coach of Australia and Daley for Channel 9.

As a recent great of the game in Australia, you aren't required or expected to fade away quietly or sit brooding sourly on your own. The game is big enough to have room for you, although the transition is easier for some than for others. Take Allan Langer, for instance. Great player and a likeable little larrikin of a bloke, loved a laugh, a punt and a beer – and still does. Hardly an obvious candidate for the often grim-faced business of modern coaching, but that's what he wants to do and he will probably get his chance. It's one of the consolations of growing old in what might loosely be called this business of writing about rugby league that, as you gradually get out of the same age bracket of current players, you find the world is increasingly full of ex-players you're glad to see again. You start off roughly the same age as the players, become the same age as the coach and eventually the same as the chairman. Sometime in the distant future, I will be the same age as the delegates they send off to the Rugby League Council.

It's not realistic to expect to have an awful lot in common with the devout 19-year-old Latter Day Saint, Israel Folau, but I could feel destiny funnelling us together. Now, Israel Folau is not a Mormon missionary. He will probably never be a Mormon missionary, but enough of a possibility exists to get the words 'Mormon missionary' into an intro and ensure that a feature on him gets into the paper, despite what I sense from twelve thousand miles away to be the creeping early stages of disillusionment with the World Cup. So it is imperative to speak with Israel Folau; I am warned not to expect too many jokes or tips for the Melbourne Cup. He's perfectly pleasant though, in a how-are-our-blokes-going-to-cope-with-this-monster? sort of way.

In fairness, England didn't handle Folau too badly, for a 19-year-old, 6ft 4", 17 stone centre. Unfortunately, two of his Melbourne team-mates, Billy Slater and Greg Inglis, both scored hat-tricks in a 52-4 kicking that was the worst-ever for England or Great Britain in a World Cup. It was also the second-worst defeat by Australia in any international, beaten only by the infamous 'day-trip to Sydney' humiliation of 2002, which at least came with a built-in excuse. At the Telstra Dome, the side defended naively, attacked without conviction when they had the ball, didn't get much of a break from ref Tony Archer and fell in a heap in the second half. There was one moment of pure poetry, when Inglis fielded Danny McGuire's kick deep in his own half and slipped it straight to Slater, who romped away to score at the other end. As an illustration of the difference between the two sides, as well as a vindication of the first part of Graeme Bradley's prophecy, it was just a little too perfect.

I listened to the analysis and the alibis and headed off to try to make sense of it all. It was not far from stadium to unit, from Dome to home, but I was disorientated by sheer exasperation and stormed off in the wrong direction, towards Bendigo and Ballarat – places of which I knew nothing other than that they had once found gold there, just as surely as England had mined a rich vein of dross that evening. It was raining heavily, it was blowing a gale, it was not what Ron Hill or anyone else was expecting. I was on the wrong side of the Yarra River and the streets were full of disgruntled northerners asking each other 'What was that shite?'

Sorry Melbourne, but I had it right first time. Manchester, but on a really, really bad night.

Packing into the press box at Parramatta

4

Sydney And The Proclaiming Of Australia

'There is only one thing wrong with international rugby league and it is that Australia are too bloody good.' Discuss.

That could be an interesting exam question. It could also be, especially when posed by a gloating Australian, as it was to me, an infuriating statement of the glaringly obvious. The 'Australia are Unbeatable' bandwagon was rolling downhill with an unstoppable momentum by the time I got back to Sydney. And, as if that wasn't hard enough to take, there was a lot of loose talk about this being the best Australian team ever. Time to leap onto the running-board of the juggernaut and at least try to apply the hand-brake. An exciting set of backs and some dazzling young athletes? Certainly. But the best-ever Australian team? Do me a favour.

A lot of people with a slightly longer memory than mine would, I fancy, make out a pretty convincing case for the 1963 side – the one that put 50 past Great Britain at Swinton.

They had the two Thornett brothers and a back-line of Ken Irvine, Graeme Langlands, Reg Gasnier and Peter Dimond, which looks a bit tasty. In the pack, there were at least two all-time greats in Ned Kelly (him again) and Johnny Raper, who didn't score himself, but had a hand in no less than nine tries at Station Road that day. Throw in Ian Walsh at hooker and that pit-bull, Barry Muir, at scrum-half and you surely have a team of more proven excellence than anything you could put onto the field now.

A recent poll voted the 1986 Kangaroos the best-ever, but I would go to the barricades in defence of the 1982 squad, the Invincibles who made history by winning every game on tour. How many of the class of 2008 would force their way into that team? Well, I'd find room for either Darren Lockyer or Billy Slater at full-back, ahead of Greg Brentnall – one of those Rules-trained players I was rambling on about in the last chapter. In the three-quarters, Mal Meninga, Steve Rogers and Eric Grothe from the '82 side pick themselves. I'd do what Australian selectors – and they do still, astonishingly, have selectors – often do by slotting in a player you can't bear to omit on the wing and replacing Kerry Boustead with Greg Inglis.

Don't ask me to even consider breaking up the immortal pairing of Brett Kenny and Peter Sterling at half-back, but Cameron Smith has the edge over Max Krilich and Steven Price forces his way into the front row. The 1982 back-row of Rod Reddy, Wayne Pearce and Ray Price gets the nod in its entirety, but the temptation to have Israel Folau as one of the subs is irresistible – until you remember who occupied the bench for the Invincibles…..only Wally Lewis.

Let's give it a go then. An '82/'08 composite side might look something like this. We'll call them The Unfathomables, although I also like the name the famously thirsty Batley side of the 1960s carried with pride – The Unquenchables.

The Unfathomables: Lockyer; Inglis, Meninga, Rogers, Grothe; Kenny, Sterling; Young, Smith, S.Price, Reddy, Pearce, R.Price.
Substitutes: Slater, Lewis, Boyd, Civoniceva.

That's giving the modern side six places out of the seventeen and I reckon that's being generous. So let's have no more silly stuff about The Best Team Ever; just acknowledge them as far too good for anyone else at the 2008 World Cup and leave it at that.

You can almost draw the conclusion from this whole virtual selection process that a strong Manly tends to mean an exceptionally strong Australia. The Sea Eagles had five players in the 1982 tour party; in 2008, they won the Grand Final, playing a brand of rugby that made a nonsense of the usual 'Australia: effective but boring' knee-jerk, and had half a dozen representatives in the World Cup squad. Not bad for the club everyone loves to hate.

When I whinged a couple of chapters ago about there being no time to go anywhere or do anything in Sydney, I wasn't including Manly. There's always time for Manly, one of those spots that sums up Australia's unfair advantage over the rest of the world. The trip there is another of Sydney's Great Ways of Getting Places, probably the greatest of all. It would be worth living in Manly and working at Circular Quay, or vice-versa, just to have the excuse to embark on the half-hour ferry journey twice a day. You can do it in fifteen minutes by jetfoil, but why rush? People spend hundreds of dollars on cruises on Sydney Harbour, when you can't really improve on the couple of quid's worth you get on the Manly Ferry. True, it can get a little choppy as you pass the entrance between North and South Heads, but, for most of the voyage, the unhurried progress between landmarks like the Harbour Bridge, Luna Park and Taronga Park Zoo on your left and the Opera House, Woolloomooloo, Double Bay, Rose Bay and Watson's Bay on your right is pure relaxation. It was what the first explorers saw as they approached the spot where the ferry pier now stands that gave the place its name. They called it Manly Cove because the men of the local aboriginal tribe seemed remarkable for their virile masculinity. It was a cautionary thought, as we neared the wharf, that had they given the opposite impression, we could be about to drop anchor in Effeminate, New South Wales. The area's detractors – and its rugby league club's detractors – would have loved that.

There is no way of explaining that hostility without diving into the murky waters of Sydney's class divides. For a nominally egalitarian city, it has a finely calibrated sense of what is posh and what is plebeian. It is based to a large extent on postcodes. You can live in a fifty-room mansion in the Western Suburbs and still be a brave little Aussie battler or at least regard yourself as such; you can live in a cardboard box on the northern beaches that stretch up the coast from Manly and still be a bloated plutocrat. Throw in the extra provocation that Manly used to pinch all Wests' best players and you begin to see why the rivalry between the two clubs – the Silvertails and the Fibros, so called for the construction of their humble fibre-board dwellings - through the 'seventies and 'eighties remains a by-word for poisonous intensity. There are no proper Wests now, not since their merger with the slightly café-society, vaguely raffish Balmain, but followers of other clubs fill the vacuum and take up the slack by hating Manly. It goes with the territory.

Manly – 'Seven Miles from Sydney and a Thousand Miles from Care,' as it used to be advertised - is the city's original seaside resort. People used to go there for their holidays before Bali became an option and there are hints about it of a southern hemisphere Blackpool – not that there is anything wrong with that. Just about everything else is calculated to induce envy.

It has a clutch of small beaches, one of them looking down the Harbour, and a magnificent, surf-lashed one, lined with Norfolk pines, staring out to the ocean. Between those two runs The Corso, a tackily exotic mall that never fails to make me feel that I'm on my hols, whether I am or not. It's the surf, though, that has been the making of Manly. It was one of the first places where the strange, Hawaiian hobby of riding the waves on an ironing board caught the Australian imagination. Its Surf Lifesaving Club claims to have been the first in the world. When I rented a unit there a few years ago, it came complete with surf-boards, but not, sadly, with the balance and co-ordination needed to stay in control of one.

When the manly men of Manly are not surfing, the chances are that they are taking part in some other sport. It's a place which demands that you get out of doors and do something – and so the perfect setting for a little experiment that the Pom author, Richard Beard, carried out in 2005. Sick of seeing British teams in a variety of sports lose to Australia, he decided to take on the Aussies at their own game – or their own games – on their own turf. For his book *Manly Pursuits*, he installed himself there and challenged the locals in a range of disciplines, including bowls, shooting, golf, swimming, surfing and running. Results were mixed, but the moral of the story was that just about everyone in Manly was playing something or other. It's no wonder they have tended to be fairly useful.

Only the athletic elite play rugby league, of course, but the sheer scale of participation is the key there as well. Lee Addison is another Manly Pom – by which I don't mean to compliment him on his masculinity – who filled a wide spectrum of roles in rugby league in England before trying his luck on the peninsula. At various times, he was Wigan's media manager, coach of the England Students' and Women's teams and, best of all, loose forward for Bolton Mets. He now coaches a junior club in the local competition and admits that his motivation, apart from living reasonably close to paradise, was to find the magic formula which enables Australia to churn out so many outstanding players. After two years, he has come to a surprising conclusion which raises the question of whether his journey was strictly necessary.

'There is no magic formula. There is no secret key. They don't do anything we don't do in England. It's all about numbers. If one boy doesn't develop as you were expecting, there's another ten coming along behind,' he says. And the one who drifts off will probably turn out to be an infuriatingly brilliant surfer or flat-green bowler.

So that, apart from a hundred restaurants, with dirt-cheap seafood the obvious speciality, is Manly. But there is something different about Manly – and even about the Manly Ferry - this particular day. Knockabout blokes who would normally be comfortable in singlet, shorts and thongs are sweltering and swaying in three-piece suits. Women who live in track suits and bikinis are tottering on six-inch heels, resplendent and very, very drunk in diaphanous dresses and elaborate hats or the twitching antennae known as fascinators. There is no sign of anyone, apart from bar-staff, doing any work of any kind. Of course....it's Melbourne Cup day.

I've always been singularly unimpressed by the Cup's claim to be The Race that Stops Australia, because that is hardly a difficult trick to pull off. In my limited experience, all you have to do to stop Australia is to whisper quietly in its ear that there could be a horse-race somewhere in the world and that it might be an idea to knock off for the day and have a punt and a beer. Australia stops then, just as though someone has flicked a switch. The Race that Starts Australia – that would be a prouder boast.

The Melbourne Cup has undeniably expanded its sphere of influence, however. Back in Phar Lap's day, it merely used to stop Melbourne. Then it stopped Victoria and eventually the whole of Australia, earning the alternative title of The Celebration that Stops a Nation. Soon it will stop the world – in case anyone wants to get off – and slow down our neighbouring planets in the Solar System. It is a big deal and everybody in Australia wants a slice of it.

On my last trip, I'd been at Randwick Races on Melbourne Cup day. They put on a programme of races to celebrate the race that is going on elsewhere, followed by the main event on the big screen. You can see the connection there, but putting on your best gear to watch it in a pub in Manly is pushing it a stage further. The Manly Wharf Hotel is so full that, by the time you battle your way to the bar, order a few pints of champagne and battle your way back, it's too late to get a bet on and we have to invest all our hopes in a humble sweepstake. For the record, the 2008 Melbourne Cup was won, just by half a nostril, by an animal called Viewed. Obviously, that was not the name on my ticket, or I would now be living in comfortable retirement somewhere in the Manly area. Peering through a waving forest of fascinators, I could never actually see my horse set off, let alone finish. To be truthful, I can't vouch for the Melbourne Cup halting absolutely everything in Australia in its stride, but it was enough to render my chosen nag stationary.

There could be a bit of a rort involved, though. I thought I would check with my Cheltenham-based racing advisor just where the Melbourne Cup, as a two-mile handicap, is considered to stand in global terms.

'Not a very good race, not usually won by a very good horse,' he harrumphed dismissively. 'Doesn't rank in the top twenty-five races of the year on my radar. Certainly not as big as the Cambridgeshire. More of a social occasion.' So there you have it – outgunned by a race that doesn't even stop Cambridge, but don't let that spoil the party.

If there is a more evocative place-name in Sydney than Manly, it must surely be Bondi Beach. Despite the rise of Coogee and the shiny, fresh appeal of recent upstarts like Darling Harbour, it is still the strongest magnet pulling in the first-time visitor. It was where I headed for when I first arrived almost thirty years ago and millions of others, before and since, have trodden the same path. Perhaps it's something in the name itself – the rhythm, the music and the alliteration of it. It just sounds right.

Of course, not everyone is impressed. On the 2004 Tri-Nations tour, Great Britain's Leon Pryce infamously compared Bondi unfavourably with Blackpool. Absurdly, that was enough to have him followed around for the next week by outraged camera crews, on his scent like the inquisition in pursuit of a heretic. Leon wasn't making the same mistake in the World Cup. He simply would not be drawn on the relative merits of any other localities - like Manly and Morecambe or St. Kilda and St. Helens. That meant that he upset nobody in Australia off the field. Unfortunately, he didn't upset anyone on the field either, but that's another story. He didn't answer many tricky questions off the pitch, or ask many on it.

As someone who has lived in both places, I could just about have gone along with Leon's preference for Blackpool if he had been talking about the Bondi of the early 'eighties. It was a tired type of a place then, living off its name and not much else, but a few things have happened since. They've closed the sewage outlet on the north headland, tarted up the promenade for the Olympic beach volleyball, restored many of the art-deco buildings and, like a lot of places in Sydney, allowed cafes and restaurants to spill out all over the pavements.

On this particular day, I'm dining at a pavement café with John, an old mate from Hong Kong days who has been living the Australian dream for twenty-odd years. Today, he is going to do two things he has never done before; he is going to have a drink in his local pub and he is going to a rugby league match.

Now, John is not one of those bizarre people who hate all sports. He has flown aerobatics competitively, he watches tennis and follows cricket obsessively – supporting Australia, I'm sorry to say, although I suppose he has the excuse of now being a citizen of his adopted country. But one sport to which he has remained stubbornly resistant, despite regular goading from me, is rugby league.

Likewise the pub. John likes a drink as much as the next man – even, let's be honest here, rather more than the next man. For twenty years, he has lived around the corner from a perfectly good pub, but he has not so much as taken the froth off a middy in there. The trouble is that it is very much a working class boozer, where blokes come in after work – except on Melbourne Cup day, of course - in their sweat and grit, swig out of the bottle, put on their bets in the TAB in the corner and play the pokies. There are seats out on the pavement, but there might be size eleven work-boots up on them. It can be a bit loud and lairy and there's probably been a fight or two there over the years. It's full of the sort of folk you might meet at a rugby league match, in other words.

I've told John that he is only buying into part of the Australian dream and is blanking out some of the best bits.

Down And Under

He must overcome his terror of working-class Australia and, over our oysters and avocado with a well-chilled Sauvignon Blanc at Bondi, he promises to try.

We make a good start, not quite in, but very adjacent to the Concord Hotel. I bring us a couple of bottles of Cooper's Sparkling Ale; he goes in, all the way to the bar, and gets us a couple more. We sit, a couple of hundred yards from his re-built house, and watch the world go by. 'I quite like it here,' he says.

And this isn't just a sneaky afternoon beer we're having here. This is important work on behalf of the Australian economy. Here, as in Britain, street-corner boozers are doing it tough. I've already noticed a number of landmarks in Sydney that have closed down and now either stand sad and empty, have been recycled as twee eateries or, in the most extreme examples, as branches of McDonald's. Every sly grog in a Sydney pub that you can squeeze into the day's busy schedule is a howl of protest against this doleful trend. Use it or lose it, John.

You know, I think I've convinced him. I have this refreshing image now of him occasionally putting off chores like feeding the cats and adjusting a new propeller to nip down the Concord for a couple of stubbies and a yarn about the footy. And what better time to start than now, whilst his partner, Jan, is away at her conference? (That's a line I thought I had better throw in, as I might have given the impression, with the cats and everything, that he's a bit gay, there being a fair amount of that mullarkey in Sydney.)

While we're at it, the RSLs could do with a helping hand as well. RSL, I hear you whimper, what impenetrable new thicket of initials is this you're dragging us through? Well, after the leagues clubs and the surf life-saving clubs, the Returned Servicemen's League forms the third column that holds up the canopy that is Sydney club-life. You used to get an RSL cab to the RSL club. You still can, but you might have further to travel with the meter running, because for the first time I saw on this trip the sight of clubs abandoned and boarded-up, the manicured bowling greens, where men in proper tailored shorts and long socks once rolled their woods, overgrown with weeds. I suppose they have simply run short of returned servicemen. Short of starting another World War, I can't really see how we can help. That's someone else's job anyway; I have a pub-going, league-watching Aussie to construct, from the most unpromising of raw materials.

We are doing really well. Down through the Korean enclave of Strathfield, out onto the Great Western Highway, past the old Western Suburbs strongholds of Lidcombe and Auburn, through Granville and down into Parramatta, John gives a convincing impression of a man looking forward to his first rugby league match. We're within sight of the ground, with supporters of both sides wending their way, when, quite suddenly, his nerve goes. 'You know what,' he says. 'I don't think I can go through with this.'

There's a lot of guff about forgetting to feed the cats, needing to re-set the lawn sprinklers or sandpaper that new propeller, but I reckon he was spooked by the sheer size of the Samoan supporters. Now, the Samoan players are big, but they are one of the few sides in rugby league history to be so heavily out-weighed by their fans. I think John had premonitions of his skinny frame being accidentally crushed between two of them in the stand. I was probably expecting too much on one day, with both the pub and the match. We'll have another go next time.

Realistically, it is the players of Ireland who should be spooked by the prospect of rubbing shoulders with the Samoans. Man for man, they cannot match the islanders, neither physically nor in terms of the standard at which they generally play. It looks a bit like NRL versus National League One, so there should really be no doubt about the outcome. There is something a bit special, though, about the spirit in this Irish side, something that is illustrated – literally – by the Gaelic tattoo that they have all had done since the defeat by Tonga. It reads: 'Without Unity There is no Strength.'

At a stroke, Ireland have declared the philosophy by which they aspire to be judged and stolen the clothes of the Samoans – the World Cup's most tattooed team. League players these days love their tattoos, but I haven't heard anything about England going down to the local parlour together to all have 'Without Unity There is no Strength' needled into their skin. 'You couldn't get that lot out for a cup of tea together,' says one mischievous Anglo-Irishman. Ah, the humour of the Irish. They've got it off Pat, as my wife, proud of her own Irish heritage, once put it.

What the Irish got off Pat – Richards of that ilk – at the Parramatta Stadium was an excellent start with the first of his three tries. The Wigan winger kicked erratically and still finished with 22 points on the ground where he used to play as a kid, as they outplayed Samoa to win 34-16, lead the group and go into the semi-final qualifier. The tattooed quasi-Irish of County Wigan and County Halifax are one game away from playing Australia. Richards, one of the better qualified players with two Dublin-born parents, is set upon at one stage by disgruntled Samoan supporters from precisely the area of the ground where John would have been if his nerve hadn't snapped. He has missed a real experience, I tell him later.

I think I've worked out what is wrong with Samoa. With players like Matt Utai, Nigel Vagana, the Puletuas and the two cleverest ball-handlers in Super League in David Solomona and Ali Lauitiiti, they should have strolled into the semis. Their failure to do so is due in large part to an unfortunate addiction. More than any other nation, they are hooked on the big hit. Like any addiction, it is all a case of too much of a good thing. After all, you want your players to hit hard in the tackle; you just don't want it to become an all-embracing obsession. You don't want them to be so keen on lining up the mighty collision that they would secretly rather not have the ball, which is a suspicion that sometimes crosses your mind when you watch Polynesian sides. And you definitely don't want them settling into a rhythm of Big Hit, Big Hit, Miss – and preferring that to the less exciting pattern of Tackle, Tackle, Tackle.

These are issues that have a resonance far beyond the World Cup, because rugby league in Australia, as in New Zealand, is more Polynesian than it ever was; you only have to look at the names in lower grades and junior competitions for confirmation of that. On the one hand, that has to be a good thing. It keeps numbers up, ensures that some much-changed areas of Sydney, for instance, remain rugby league hotbeds and guarantees a flow of the commodity that the game will always need – big, young athletes.

On the other hand – and people tip-toe around the racial minefield that it is possible to wander into here – it has changed the nature of the game. It is not just that Polynesians are bigger, they are bigger younger than their contemporaries from other ethnic groups. That makes life in the junior ranks awfully tough for a scrawny, blond-haired half-back, let alone a Korean, Vietnamese or Cambodian kid, to name three nations well represented in these parts, having to battle with lads of the same age but approximately twice the size.

The recent replacement rules have made matters worse. It wouldn't be too bad facing Iafeta Paleaaesina – to quote an extreme example – for the fifteen minutes for which he is effective, if you could also run at him and round him for the sixty-five for which he isn't. But no, you can't do that, because by that time his coach will have brought on another, fresher Feka, followed by another couple, by which time the original is well rested and ready to batter you again. You can't blame lads for being big and strong, but it can distort the game and make it very one-dimensional and predictable.

Predictable, that is, when they are not put on their behinds by compact forwards like Eamonn O'Carroll, Bob Beswick and Michael McIlorum. None of them, nor any of their team-mates, is ever going to frighten anyone when they walk into a room. They are typical rugby players with average physiques and solid CVs who found something extra when they needed it. Likewise, Andy Kelly wouldn't claim to be cutting edge technically as a coach, having spent most of his career in the lower divisions. But he found a way in the World Cup of grafting that something extra onto his players. Witnessing his pride in his team, it was impossible not to reflect on the adversity he has known in his own life, particularly his fight against cancer. He knows how tough times can make you tougher. It wouldn't surprise me if he had had a crafty word with the tattoo artist that week. 'Make it hurt a bit. Not too much, but enough for them to remember.'

On the face of it, Scotland were in line for a painful experience of their own that same night. Even more than Ireland, they were an unashamed patchwork of odds and sods and they were up against a Fijian side that had been a revelation against France. It's a fascinating story, Fijian rugby league, revolving as it does around the tropical paradise of Rochdale. That town's Hornets were the first club to sign Fijian players in the early 'sixties and Rochdale became the destination of choice for a succession of players, regardless of who had recruited them. For a while, they all lived in a big, communal house together on the outskirts of town. If you bought a map of Britain in Suva, it would have London and Edinburgh in normal-sized script and ROCHDALE in big, red block capitals. There is now a community of close to a hundred Fijians in their unofficial capital of England. They have a Fijian Association and go to Blackpool and Southport for weekends together by the sea, which must be just like going home. They also play rugby.

I noticed recently that Mike Ratu, the third generation of player of that name to operate out of Rochdale, so he, strictly speaking, is Mike Ratu Jnr Jnr, had been re-signed by Leeds after a season on loan at Halifax. When I went to see them, they were in training for the Carnegie Nines at Headingley and also hoping that a few of them were in line for a call-up for the World Cup. They weren't, but only because Joe Dakuitoga – ex-Sheffield – was spoilt for choice closer to home. Not only are there players like Jarryd Hayne and Wes Naiqama playing in the NRL, but there are men of Fijian birth or heritage doing their thing all over Australia. Their World Cup squad included players from Terrigal, Milton-Ulladulla, Fassifern, Sawtell and Darlington Point, as well as from one of Australia's better-named country clubs, the Parkes Spacemen. And I bet they all know the way to Rochdale.

Seeing how they shaped up against Scotland was just a matter of side-stepping Ireland's celebrations at their nearby hotel and crossing the car park to Parramatta Leagues Club; caps to be removed, bags to be left at reception, lest they contain caps we might be tempted to put on in the excitement of the moment. The match from Gosford is on in the Peter Sterling Bar, a fitting tribute to a player who remains one of the all-time greats in my book. I'll swear that some of the honorary Irish who have just cheered them to victory have become honorary Scots, having put something borrowed and blue on top of their green.

They were about to see something remarkable; another example of the mystery that is the whole adding up to more than the sum of the individual parts. Not that those individual parts were rubbish; not with players like Brough, the three Hendersons and Michael Robertson, fresh from scoring a hat-trick of tries in Manly's Grand Final victory. The player who best summed up their effort, however, was Iain Morrison, London-born but a proud Scot – and capable of winning a Mick Cassidy look-alike contest, even if Cass himself entered.

The Scots hung in doggedly against the Bati – as Fijian warriors are known – but fell behind near the end to Semi Tadulala's second try. They were not going to win by the 28 points needed to reach the semi-finals, but a first-ever World Cup victory was still within their reach. It was grasped when Oliver Wilkes crashed over and Brough landed the conversion for an 18-16 scoreline. They were not exactly dancing a strathspey in the streets of McParramatta, but there were a few choruses of *Flower of Scotland*, or the Henderson Brothers' re-mix, 'Flower of Torquay.'

Time was running out in Sydney, but the Scottish theme was to reverberate all the way to check-out. I always have this distinct pang of regret when I leave the place, with the question of when and if I'll be back hanging in the air like an un-defused bomb over a nervous full-back. It can be a tough, hard-nosed old joint beneath the picture-postcard surface, but, as a second home, it takes a bit of beating. Were I to be re-incarnated as a Sydneysider, even one who doesn't much care for rugby league, there would be few complaints from this quarter.

There's rather an odd duty to be performed before this particular departure. Like a feckless parent who has missed a string of his or her children's birthdays, the ARL is playing World Cup catch-up by deciding on a Man of the

Tournament for every competition since 1954. Hence this convening of an 'expert' panel in one of Sydney's half-million coffee shops. Now, some of you will be well aware that I can't always be relied upon to get this sort of thing right when the match is still going on right in front of me, so what chance have I got after half a century?

Fortunately, the first name we have to come up with is childishly easy if you keep your Caledonian connections in mind. Dave Valentine was a craggy Scot from Hawick, who played with distinction for Huddersfield, captained Great Britain in the 1954 World Cup in France and became the first man to lift the trophy.

It wasn't easy. If any member of the 2008 England squad ever feels like having a moan over any aspect of their campaign, he should take a long look at the arrangements fifty-four years before. They had no coach once they left home, no preparation to speak of and most of their better players declined to take part after a gruelling Ashes tour. Transport and accommodation were chaotic, no doubt the steak was raw and there was no juicy cash bonus on offer for winning the Cup. Yet Valentine – and those who were there are adamant that it was largely down to his leadership and personality – managed to weld this bits and pieces selection into a tournament-winning side.

Not even the Australians on the panel could argue against him as Player of the Tournament, but I also like the story of another Scot who established a tradition which I hoped would re-surface in 2008 by becoming one of 1954's unlikely heroes. The Leeds winger, David Rose, was woken up at his mother's home in Jedburgh by the village bobby, who told him that Billy Boston had pulled out through injury and his country needed him. Rose rode the milk train over the border and played in all four games in France, scoring four tries, including one in the final.

Likewise, I couldn't argue against Brian Carlson in 1957, because his is one of the great World Cup stories. His country club in Queensland, Blackall, didn't want him to play and when he insisted on doing so they promptly sacked him. Carlson, playing the tournament as a free agent, was the key man behind Australia's first World Cup win.

In 1960, the British selectors got around the insoluble problem of having three world-class loose forwards by playing all three of them – Johnny Whiteley, Vince Karalius and Derek Turner – whenever they could. As a nine-year-old, I just leaned towards Karalius as the most influential of the three; we talked of little else at Marsh Lane Primary. The froth was barely off the cappuccinos and we had two British winners. Talk about on a roll, a brie and bacon roll, to be precise.

Ron Coote and Bobby Fulton took the next two titles, followed by another British automatic choice – Clive Sullivan. The great Welsh wingman matched Valentine by taking a team to France that was given little chance and leading them to victory. He even scored that unforgettable length-of-the-field try in the final in Lyon to enable Great Britain to draw 10-10 with Australia and win the trophy on count-back. It's a sobering thought that, way back in 1972, he became and remains the last British captain to lift any silverware that really mattered – if that doesn't sound disrespectful to series wins over New Zealand. Valentine and Sullivan had something else in common; they both died young, well before their time, as, by a less dramatic margin, did Vince Karalius, later in 2008. Just the sound of those three names seemed inspiring as we mulled over their achievements.

After that, it was just a matter of nodding through a succession of Australians: Arthur Beetson, Mick Cronin, Wally Lewis, Mal Meninga, Andrew Johns and Wendell Sailor.

Great players all – well, nearly all – but, as genuine World Cup icons, I don't think you can look past our fellows. To paraphrase the old West Indies cricket calypso, those much-missed heroes of mine, Karalius, Sullivan and Valentine.

But there's a honking of the horn and the revving of an engine to remind me that the bus is impatient to leave – and to take us to the corner of Australia where Clive Sullivan, for one, should have felt most at home.

Down And Under

Dave Woods interrupts my impersonation of a
gargoyle with a stray elbow

5

Newcastle And The Reframing Of Australia

Newcastle's number one citizen, Andrew Johns, claims in his brutally honest autobiography, *The Two of Me*, that his home-town is simultaneously the most laid-back and the most proudly parochial in Australia.

Either half of that proposition would qualify as 'a big statement', because there are some pretty one-eyed and parochial places in this country and many that are so laid-back as to be horizontal. The only way to achieve excellence in both categories is to have a split personality – something to which the greatest player of his day himself admits. If Newcastle shares the same violent contrast of moods, it is no wonder he feels at home there.

Anyone of his Welsh heritage really ought to. Johns's great-grandfather came from Wales to work in the coalmines of the Hunter Valley; his Grandad worked in the seams of Australia's richest field of black coal and so did his dad. If Wales had reached the World Cup finals, instead of falling on their shovels against the Scots, this would have been the logical place for them to have been based.

There is something reminiscent of Richard Burton reading *Under Milk Wood* in the way Ron Hill intones the Welsh place-names off the road-signs as we approach the city. 'Cardiff…. Swansea…. Gresford…. Toronto….' Yes, I know Toronto isn't generally considered a Welsh place-name, but in a Sunday-best Tiger Bay accent, it sounds like one.

If they aren't producing echoes of the Welsh Valleys, the road directions threaten to re-route you to the north-east of England. Gosford…. Hexham…. Morpeth…. Gateshead…. Stockton…. Wallsend…. Lambton…. Newcastle itself. 'It's to remind you all of the Old Dart,' says the coach driver.

If that means nothing to you, don't worry about it. I wrote a column called The Old Dart for fifteen years and I never knew what it meant. Well, I knew it meant England, but I didn't know why and no-one in Australia can tell you. After extensive research, I can reveal that it has nothing to do with Dartmoor Prison, nothing to do with the arrows that cartoon convicts wore on their uniforms and even less to do with any fanciful notions that, from certain angles, England is shaped a little like a dart, with Cornwall as the pointy bit. No, the best theory I can come up with is that it is a corruption of the Old Dirt, used to denote the Old Country, in the same way that the Irish might refer to the Ould Sod – by which they do not mean Mick Cassidy. Why change the I to an A? Not a clue, apart from the Australian compulsion to do strange things to the language.

Newcastle was originally known as Coal River and one of the worst things that could happen to you as a convict, apart from being flogged to death, was to be sent there to work in the mines. The industry was in full swing by 1830 and was a major employer in the city until the 1960s, when the old pits near the coast shut down, just as they were doing in the Old Dart – perfectly logically, given the forthcoming abundance of hassle-free alternative energy sources, like nuclear power, Middle Eastern oil and Russian gas. The major local customer disappeared when the steelworks closed in 1999 – although its remains still loom over the city. But that wasn't quite the end of the story of taking coals to and from Newcastle. There are still extensive workings further inland, at places like Kurri Kurri and Cessnock – where Andrew Johns and his brother, Matthew, grew up – enough to make Newcastle still the biggest coal-exporting port in the world. Some of it probably goes to South Wales and Co. Durham.

Cessnock is about twenty miles up the Hunter Valley, which is a lot more famous these days for another product. Along with the Barossa Valley in Victoria and the Southern Vales near Adelaide, the Hunter is Australia's premier wine-producing area as well as its oldest. There are one hundred and forty wineries in the Lower Hunter alone, from tiny one and two-man operations to internationally known names like Lindeman, McGuigan and Wyndham Estate. Nearly all of them offer tastings at the cellar door, although it is not a good idea to attempt all one hundred and forty in a single afternoon. It is also a beautiful part of the world, with rolling hills and paddocks dotted with horses stopping the vineyards from all merging together. You wouldn't know that the earth beneath is honeycombed by old mine-workings; perhaps that is what gives the Hunter Valley's Semillions their distinctive flavour.

Coal and wine, it is an unusual combination, as though the Rhonda, in its grime-black hey-day, had also started knocking out a cheeky Chardonnay. It is a blend that has left the valley and the city close by not quite sure whether they are Castleford or Tuscany, Middlesbrough or Rio de Janeiro.

Down And Under

When we saw the part of town in which we were staying, there was another suggestion. 'Looks more like bloody Beirut' – surely a bit of an exaggeration, even though the pub across the road had been burnt-out fairly recently and was now just a blackened, empty shell. At first, I thought that the Ducks Nuts further down the street had suffered the same fate, but in their case it was more of a deliberate style statement. The look is very Newcastle – post-industrial bohemian – and the clientele very mixed. The landlord confides that he is thinking of reverting to the pub's staid original name, the Family and Commercial Hotel, because he wonders whether the Ducks Nuts – with its signs showing a well-endowed waterfowl on a surfboard - attracts the wrong mob and puts off a more refined crowd. 'I think you might lose more than you gain,' I tell him. The Ducks Nuts turns out to be something of a life-saver over the next few days, given that the room in our hotel is barely big enough to share with a folded-up copy of *The Guardian*, let alone the reporter from *The Guardian*.

There is an even rougher pub a little further down the street, but I never crossed that threshold. As the door swung open, you could hear the unmistakable sounds of hand-to-hand combat within, but I wasn't allowed to join in. I was improperly dressed for bar-room brawling in flip-flops with no socks and therefore turned away. Thank heavens someone is maintaining standards.

One thing Newcastle has always maintained is its unswerving loyalty to rugby league. Perhaps that is why, even though most of the industry has gone, it still feels such a working-class town. It has its roots firmly intact and rugby league is one of the firmest of them. Newcastle was the first place outside the Sydney area to which the new game came, just as if everybody instinctively knew that it would prove fertile ground. In 1908, it became the first venue outside

Sydney to host an international when Newcastle twice played the New Zealand All Golds – once under union rules and once at the new code. Newcastle lasted just two seasons in the Sydney Premiership. That was not because the game hadn't taken off in the city, but because it had taken off so well that it graduated to its own, four-team competition, which eventually grew to ten. The problem for Newcastle was that, at around one hundred miles north, it is an awkward distance from Sydney; not quite close enough to be in its competition as it was constituted before the early-'eighties, but close enough for its best players to gravitate there. Among those who followed that route were many people's choice as the greatest of all Australian players, Clive Churchill, Brian Carlson of 1957 World Cup fame, Les Johns (no relation), John Sattler and hundreds of lesser-known names.

Despite that constant drain on its resources, Newcastle sustained a vibrant local competition and enjoyed memorable victories over some distinguished touring teams. They beat New Zealand in 1913, Great Britain in 1936 and 1946, plus the series-winning 1955 French. It is a remarkable record and a reminder of how loudly the heart of rugby league beats in this town – but Newcastle's destiny lay in mixing it with the big boys in the premier domestic competition. Nobody is a better illustration of how well they have done that than the man we are about to run into in the smart part of town.

Like everywhere in the world that can do so, Newcastle has redeveloped its manky old industrial water-front as the place to eat and drink. From this one, you can look across the bay and take in surfers and coal-freighters in the same glance. I had the best meal of the whole trip at a restaurant on the jetty – and anyone who knows how well the average Australian eats will appreciate what a huge statement that is – and almost next-door is the brewery tap for Bluetongue, the local beer, where Malcolm Reilly is holding court. Malcolm is Newcastle royalty; now that he is unaccountably out of the game, he chooses to live there, rather than either of the other places where he enjoys similar status – Castleford and Manly. If there is one thing that guarantees you beatification in Australian rugby league, it is being instrumental in a club's first Premiership. Malcolm has been the driving force behind two. In 1970, the Manly boss, Ken Arthurson saw him play with such passion and desire in Great Britain's Ashes-winning side and recognised him as the missing ingredient that could win them a Grand Final. In 1972, he did so, with his unique blend of refined skills and utter ruthlessness giving the Sea Eagles the edge. The Newcastle Knights came into what was then the Winfield Cup in 1988 and were soon highly competitive. They had to send for a Pom to win it though and, in fairness, Malcolm Reilly did not inherit a bad squad of players.

I remember going to see him after he arrived in 1994, when he was still like a kid in a toy-shop, excited by the array of talent at his disposal – headed by the Johns boys, Robbie O'Davis, Darren Albert and company, but also including a player he regarded as even more talented than the brothers, in one Jamie Ainscough.

Not that his relationship with Andrew was always an easy one. I wouldn't have minded being a fly on the wall when Malcolm told him he was a lair, a hoon and a dead-set boofhead after he went off the rails on more than one occasion.

There's a theory about scrum-halves that all the great ones have had some demon snapping at their heels, be it booze, drugs, gambling or just a general anger with the world. Look at all the best ones and they usually have at least one of those chewing away at them. Conversely, think of good number sevens who have been perfectly solid citizens and well-balanced members of society. Isn't there something missing? A bit of devil, perhaps? Andrew Johns, as we now know, had most of the above problems and a few more besides. A great, great player – many good judges' best-ever – but clearly something wrong with him as well. He has since been diagnosed with bi-polar disorder, which used to carry the more familiar name of manic depression, a condition which can keep you spiraling between the highest of highs and the most desperate of lows. Throw the pills and the beer – not much of a wine drinker, fortunately – into the mixer and it's a bit of a mystery how he functioned at all, let alone played model professionals off the park week after week. But would he have been a better player as a sober, straitlaced individual on a permanent even keel? No, he would not. He's a bit like Newcastle, not quite sure whether to be exuberant, depressed or both – and not easy to change without bringing the demolition men in, although the earthquake in 1989 had a good try.

Malcolm Reilly got the best out of the player even his own family call 'Joey' in the 1997 season and the Knights famously won the comp, with Johns laying on the winning try with a visionary pass for Darren Albert as time ran out against Manly. Admittedly, there will always be an asterisk alongside that Grand Final in the record books, because that was the year of the notorious split competition in the midst of the Super League wars.

But, a word of advice here, do not stand up in the Ducks Nuts or anywhere similar and declare that there was anything tainted about that first Premiership. They might be parochial and laid-back, but they aren't big believers in asterisks in Newcastle. As far as they're concerned, Roy Asterisk is a big Kiwi prop who was ruled out of the World Cup by injury. End of story.

After Newcastle, it is hardly surprising that Reilly

struggled to teach players at Huddersfield how to pass and catch the ball. The talent he had worked with had spoiled him for that. You can't run into him, though, without reflecting on his six years as Great Britain coach – six years that included some memorable victories and some frustrating near-misses. I won't kid you that it was always a carefree, idyllic experience covering Great Britain when Malcolm and Maurice Lindsay were in charge, but it would set you up for anything the future might throw at you. If you've survived Malcolm Reilly's long, hard stare after writing something he didn't like, you're not going to be fazed by anything any future national coach might say or do – and I don't recall a lot of players messing him about either.

I remember a lot of the distinctive features of his time in charge – the arm-wrestling contests, the under-water swimming challenges, the under-water arm-wrestling – but one interesting contrast with the current regime was over the matter of who slept where. Malcolm and Maurice used to think long and hard over rooming arrangements.

Traditionally, only the captain on tour gets a room to himself; the rest have to double up. Getting the pairings right is as tricky as it is in the Ryder Cup. Some basic principles apply: no established club couples; introvert with extrovert; brash young prop with wise old prop – that sort of thing. It's also a good idea to pair-up two players who are going to be working a good deal together, but don't really know each other; a new pair of half-backs, for instance. That's what they did with Garry Schofield and Bobbie Goulding and they are big mates to this day. Mind you, Bobbie did finish that tour in the police cells, so maybe they are not the best advert for the science of room selection. Read any player's autobiography – even Andrew Johns' – and the topic of room-mates always comes up, even if it is only in the form of a complaint about snoring, farting or leaving sweaty jock-straps lying about the gaff. Rooming with a relative stranger is part of the tour experience, but England chose to ignore the Wisdom of the Ages and let the players choose. Surprise, surprise – they chose to shack up with team-mates from their clubs, thus gaining nothing for the squad in terms of breaking down cliques or mixing and matching personalities. 'What was that all about?' asked the Ireland captain, Scott Grix, contrasting the spirit in the two squads after the tournament was over. What indeed. Tony Smith has been a teacher, so he must know that if you let a class sit as they please, all the loud and disruptive kids will cluster together, as will the quiet, frightened kids, and the chemistry lab will burn down. At least, it did in my schooldays.

From what I saw, I don't believe some of the sillier stuff that came out of the England camp during the World Cup. It was not exactly a prison camp, not Guantanamo Bay by a long chalk. Nor was there any total ban on drinking. I didn't see any players dead-drunk in doorways or acting like arseholes at airports, as I have on previous tours, and I call that progress. Mind you, we never faced the real test of our ability to keep a lid on the booze, because the usual trigger – that of beating Australia – was never pulled. It's not the only reason why we never beat Australia twice in quick succession, but going on a bender for several days is certainly one of the reasons.

You don't want to go to the opposite extreme of locking players in their hotel and boring them to death; groups of players did go out for a quiet beer and were far from surreptitious about it. So far, so good. Maybe I was unlucky, though, because I only ever saw either a gang of St. Helens (or ex-St. Helens) players or a gang of Leeds (or ex-Leeds) players, never a mixture of the two. I don't believe there was active hostility between the two factions, in the sense of fights or obvious arguments, but it hardly smacks of breaking down club cliques and developing the special sort of unity that makes teams over-achieve.

Just as well, then, that England only had to play such a piss-poor Kiwi team. Let me rephrase that slightly: only had to play a New Zealand side with such apparent deficiencies and so much more notable for those who were not playing, rather than for those who were. At the root of those shortcomings was the lack of the sort of blue-chip, dominant player the Kiwis had been able to call upon in the recent past; players like Stacey Jones, Ruben Wiki, Richie Barnett and Stephen Kearney, now the coach but still much missed on the field.

On top of that, there was the slow drain to rugby union, which had claimed a potentially match-winning left-wing combination of Shontayne Hape and Lesley Vainikolo, as well as the most damaging loss of all, that of Sonny Bill Williams. It's a maddening case. Williams is a classic example of a boofhead, who was convinced by his 'advisors' that he would be better off out on a limb on his own, in a country where he doesn't speak the language, playing a game he knows nothing about. The quality of the 'advice' he was getting is characterised by the absence of the rather important snippet of information that he needed a visa to get into France. That meant days of playing hide and seek with the Australian and New Zealand media in London, before he could get to Toulon and promptly get injured. He'll finish up in Super League one day, but he probably hasn't behaved quite badly enough yet. His woeful injury record means that we will never know how good he could have been at rugby league; the galling thing is that, when he produced one of his occasional big games, he looked potentially the best forward you had ever seen in your life. Oh well, c'est la vie, as they say down Belmore way.

Of course, I'm assuming here that he would have chosen to play for New Zealand, had he stayed in rugby league, rather than exercising one of his inevitable other options. That was the other drain on the Kiwis' strength – players deciding on an alternative nationality for the World Cup. They included Ali Lauitiiti, David Solomona, Kylie Leuluai, Francis Meli, Willie Talau, Matt Utai, the Puletua brothers and Nigel Vagana, who all elected to play for Samoa. Half a Kiwi side there and Tonga had some pretty useful candidates as well – including the still inactive Fuifui Moimoi.

Kearney also opted against calling up more than a token presence from Super League, leaving out veterans like the Paul brothers and consistent performers like Paul Whatuira. Then there's the relatively mundane business of injuries, which just happened to deprive the Kiwis of their two remaining players of incontrovertible world class – Brent Webb and Roy Asotasi (not to be confused with Roy Asterisk). What did that leave? Not a lot, with a particular fault-line running through the middle of the team and no really convincing contenders for full-back, stand-off, scrum-half or hooker.

Apart from that, no problems. All Kearney and his side-kick, Wayne Bennett, had to do was to fill those four rather crucial positions from a list of possibles that ran something like this: Lance Hohaia (too small); Benji Marshall (too fragile); Thomas Leuluai (too pedestrian); Nathan Fien (too Australian); Krisnan Inu (too Mormon); Isaac Luke (too random). It was like a jigsaw with several missing pieces; no matter how you shuffled it all around, there were still gaps that couldn't be filled properly.

Or that was the way it looked in Newcastle, a place I set out to know a little better as the familiar pre-match nerves started to kick in. As a means of distraction, I'd recommend a stroll to Nobby's Lighthouse; nothing to do, I should add, with the previous national coach. It has an interesting history. It began life as Nobby's Island, but it was thought that made it a little too, well, isolated. The solution to that was to chop the top off the island and create a causeway to connect it to the land, ideal for walking along before potentially ruinous rugby league internationals. From the lighthouse, you have a commanding view of the surfers, the coal-freighters, the disused steelworks, the whole panorama of Newcastle and.... Good grief, it's still only half past nine!

Another tried and tested time-killer is a swim in the ocean pool, where you can be lashed invigoratingly by surf and spray, without the inconvenient business of being swept out to sea. On the way there, however, there is a hubbub from a park on the other side of the road. The Kiwis are playing cricket – very badly – and laughing like lunatics as Wayne Bennett swipes across the line and loses all three stumps. It's not quite as it would have been in the days of coaches like Bob Bailey and Frank Endacott, who would make laid-back Novocastrians seem tightly-coiled and would probably have called us over and given us a turn at bat, but there were a couple of friendly waves and a general air of relaxation.

You couldn't help thinking how you would love to see England doing the same sort of thing. But it wouldn't happen, for two reasons: a) They wouldn't do it and b) they wouldn't want you around if they did. No-one seems to have told the Kiwis that they have won just one of their last six internationals – and that against Papua New Guinea – and are bidding, in this World Cup of superlatives, for the title of Worst Kiwi Team Ever. If anyone has told them, they don't seem too bothered. So a vague suspicion begins to take shape. Could these be the ones of whom the great sage Bradley foretold? The apparently hopeless side that will emerge triumphant in the Last Days? Nah, don't be daft.

There is a little insight on the way to the game, however, that should give long-term hope to both them and us.

The Knights' stadium is over in Lambton, so the obvious place for a pre-match gathering and a meet-up with a few stragglers from the Old Dart is Newcastle Wests Leagues Club. Wests are one of the original clubs in the local comp, the wealthiest and the one most closely involved with the birth of the Knights twenty years ago. We know that from there it's no distance to what was once Marathon and is now EnergyAustralia Stadium, but aren't quite sure of the exact direction. We ask a young chap on duty in the foyer and he is horrified. 'Which way do you do what? Walk? You couldn't walk there. I'll get you a taxi.' I must look like a pretty broken-down old wreck these days, but a pleasant ten-minute stroll gets us to the ground, once we have persuaded our mate that we aren't going to collapse half-way, dehydrated and demented like Burke and Wills trying to cross the parched interior.

I can't fully describe to you how much glee this tiny episode brings me. It's proof that Australia's effortless superiority at all things athletic could yet turn out to be a mere blip on the screen. If young men are frightened of walking for ten minutes, then the process of slobification that has made us so hopeless at so many things is well advanced here as well. The pie is destined to triumph over the pineapple and Australia will produce generations of pimply, sedentary youths, who will not be much cop at playing anything but computer games. They will not exactly be couch potatoes, more lounge lizards – because, in Australia, a lounge is what you, well, lounge on and a lounge-room is where you do it. You have to admit, it's a hopeful scenario and it might, looking at some recent Australian sports results, already be taking shape.

Waiting at the end of our half-mile epic is haka-gate.

Down And Under

Wikipedia – not to be confused with Ruben Wikipedia – defines the haka as 'a posture dance with shouted accompaniment' and it is a standard prelude to New Zealand rugby matches, both league and union. The version we are most familiar with is the one that starts with much slapping of the thighs and the opening line 'Ka mate, ka mate....' In my ignorance in the early 'eighties, it crossed my mind that it was something to do with announcing that day's line up: Tamati, Tamati, Broadhurst, Sorensen.... Were I an opposing player, I would have found that far more intimidating than some Maori phrases I didn't understand. Intriguingly, 'Ka mate' is not quite the straightforward challenge to do battle that it is usually assumed to be. It's more of a poem of renewal, about death giving way to new life, darkness to light, winter to summer. As such, it has some close equivalents in most cultures, although usually without the rolling eyes and protruding tongues.

A rough translation would go something like this:

> *'I die, I die. I live, I live.*
> *I die, I die. I live, I live*
> *This is the hairy man who brought the sun*
> *And caused it to shine again.*
> *An upward step.... Another upward step....*
> *Another upward step.... Another....*
> *And the sun shines.'*

Purists disapprove of the jump at the end, but that is now firmly established as part of the haka.

Other rugby league nations have their own versions. Tonga and Samoa, of course, as they showed to considerable theatrical effect before their meeting at Penrith. The Cook Islands, snubbed for this World Cup, have a beauty. Even Australia, fearing that they might be missing out on something, felt compelled to fabricate an aboriginal war-dance for use on tours in the 'fifties and 'sixties. It lacked the required cultural credibility and was allowed to quietly lapse. New Zealand is different; Kiwis of whatever ilk – Maori, Islander or Pakeha – all do the haka at school and there is a national familiarity with it that makes it work. Rather than gripe about any supposed psychological advantage it might give them, as other countries sometimes do, we should hit back with the weapon we have been hiding up our sleeves for too long – morris dancing.

I was reading the other day that morris – which may or may not be a corruption of 'moorish' – dancing is in danger of dying out because it is performed exclusively by beardy old blokes and anyone younger is too embarrassed to take it up. As a nation, we are uniquely easy to embarrass by any mention of our heritage of music and dance. Nobody else suffers from this. Anyone with half an egg-cup of Irish blood will be up there jigging with the best of them at the drop of a hat. Anyone with a third of a test-tube of Scots can hardly wait to don a kilt and dance a Highland fling. But show an Englishman the glories of the morris and he curls up in a ball on the floor. Well, if we're ever going to match the antipodeans in the pre-match, that has to change. I'm not thinking of the Cotswold variety, with its bells and white handkerchiefs, but something from further north, where the dancers wear clogs and attack each other with tree-branches. Or the Earlsdon sword dance, which in its purest form ends with the ritual beheading of one participant. If that doesn't get our brave boys in the mood, nothing will.

In the meantime, though, the problem remains of what to do while the opposition are celebrating their culture, rolling their eyes and sticking out their tongues. The answer that England came up with in Newcastle was to turn their backs on it all, form a huddle and talk among themselves. What we didn't realise at the time was that the English defence later that evening would be based on exactly the same tactics.

It all started so well. An England team freshened up with six players making their first World Cup appearances came flying out of the blocks with two early tries and led by 16 points after half an hour. It would have been all over if Paul Wellens had not been barged into the corner-flag with another try beckoning. Not only was the try disallowed, but the full-back was injured, something that had consequences that we could not have pictured in our worst nightmares.

There's an apparent contradiction in all this, because it wasn't as though Wellens was even playing well. Can your lack of pace catch up with you, or is that a logical absurdity? If it can, that is what had happened to Paul. Don't get me wrong, in many ways he has been one of my favourite players for the last ten years. He's one of the most likeable lads in the game, an excellent thinking footballer and a real team-man. If he'd had any pace, he would have been the best full-back you ever saw in your life – and I don't exclude Darren Lockyer and Billy Slater from that. For years, he got away with it by being fast between the ears and by reading the game so well. In fact, you have hardly ever noticed in domestic rugby that, by comparison with those two, he lacks a top gear. Every credit to him for having the football intelligence to compensate, but then, oh dear, he loses another half-a-yard and the game is up, the equation tilted just too far against him. Wellens had struggled so far in the World Cup, but there was no realistic alternative. When he got hurt, however, there was farce and chaos.

Losing a full-back is not such an unthinkable event that it should throw a team of internationals into complete confusion. From 24-8, England collapsed to 24-36 amid the worst failure of a defensive system you could ever see at this level. The record books show that Manu Vatuvei scored four tries, which suggests that the man they call The Beast bulldozed the poor old Poms. He certainly looked the part – almost as big as Vainikolo, all bulging muscles and gold teeth – but he could have scored those tries if he had all the physical presence of the least prepossessing of the Seven Dwarfs.

For three of them he never had a hand laid on him as England experimented with the non-sliding slide-defence.

It was not good enough to blame the obvious scapegoats – Paul Sykes and, to a lesser extent, Mark Calderwood – because the failure was collective and systemic. This might sound like hyperbole, but you genuinely would have torn out your hair in the Pennine League. It was not a problem of selection, either of the World Cup squad or the team on the day. From a disastrously thin field, Messrs. Sykes and Calderwood had, on form, as good a right to be there as anyone. They were not the worst defensive players Tony Smith could have picked. Indeed, Calders had played his way onto the plane with a magnificent tackling stint for Wigan at Headingley. Also, on the first-choice players' form, the fringe players had to be given a run if the selection process was to have any integrity.

Coach Smith has been blamed for the wrong things; he didn't leave better players in England and he did his homework all season on contenders' form. The trouble was that the best he could put on the field couldn't read situations and couldn't adapt to changes forced upon them. They made Lance Hohaia look like Wally Lewis as his long, looping passes kept releasing Vatuvei to canter to the line at his leisure. Nor is it much of an excuse that Isaac Luke milked the penalty that gave New Zealand the lead for the first time with a blatant dive. Two points in a 28 point collapse – hardly statistically significant. It all begged a couple of questions: How was it possible to get players to forget everything they knew about wide defence in a couple of weeks overseas? And, if we leave at three-quarter time, how quickly can we get back to Wests Leagues or even the Ducks Nuts?

Later, it transpires that we've messed up before the match, as well as during it. Benji Marshall is persuaded to complain that England had 'lacked respect' in ignoring the haka. 'The very least we expected by way of response was a bit of morris dancing,' he said, although I could have mis-heard that part. Coach Smith responds by suggesting that crossing the half-way line and sticking their tongues out could be considered ill-mannered on the part of the Kiwis. Nice to know that we might still have the edge in matters of etiquette. The organisers issue an edict that teams must not venture beyond half-way when doing the haka; unfortunately there is no such restriction once the game starts.

The result means that, despite the rigged draw, England are not guaranteed to reach the semi-finals, although it will take a thumping PNG victory over Australia to prevent it. What a laugh that would have been, if the Aussies had taken an Isaac Luke-style dive and contrived that outcome. But then that would only have made sense if they had regarded us as a threat. As it was, they won comfortably in Townsville by 46-6, but not in a way that reflected any discredit on the Kumuls.

This was one of a number of apparently one-sided games which were actually very watchable. PNG might have lost by 40 points, but they attacked and defended like their lives depended on it; in other words, and there is no way around this, they played a good deal better against Australia than England did. Stanley Gene was carried shoulder-high around Dairy Farmers Stadium after what was supposed to be his last Test; although let's give it a decade or so before we give full credence to that.

The game was also notable for the debut of the Manly winger, David Williams, popularly known at The Wolfman. I have to say that, on one level, he's a bit of a disappointment. I was expecting a display of facial hair that would put Ned Kelly to shame, but he looks less of a Wolfman than I do. His trimmed and abbreviated beard is less Noel Cleal than Rolf Harris, more Jeremy Beadle than Brian Blessed. On the other hand, he does score three tries on his first Test appearance, all of which have to be worked for and scored past a genuinely out-flanked defence, because PNG's tackling is so good and so honest.

Given an impossible task, Papua New Guinea have achieved something a little beyond impossible - losing all three of their matches but still emerging with huge credit. They leave Townsville in rather better shape than England leave Newcastle, which is a bit of a shame for those English supporters who will always think of it in association with that train-wreck of a second half, rather than as a place which, in its way, represents the best of Australia, with all its contrasts and contradictions. If someone had twenty-four hours, didn't want to do any sight-seeing and wasn't worried about a few rough edges, I'd send them, like the coals, to Newcastle.

*Britain's finest about to be swallowed by
a giant effigy of Margaret Thatcher*

6

The Gold Coast And The Playgrounds Of Australia

In 1933, the handful of inhabitants of the quiet coastal settlement of Elston took a momentous decision. They voted to request a change of name to something a little more catchy and attractive to potential visitors. Goodbye Elston; hello Surfers Paradise.

It had only ever been called Elston in the first place because the local postmaster christened it that, after his wife's hometown in Nottinghamshire, not far from Newark – an area not noted for its beach culture. It has been a spectacularly successful rebranding, because Surfers is now the focal point of what is simultaneously Australia's sixth-biggest city and its biggest holiday resort.

The Gold Coast – the generic term for the almost fifty miles of coastline between the outskirts of Brisbane and the New South Wales border – is another new name, only official since 1958. The way it has developed, its alternative title, The Concrete Coast, looks more and more appropriate.

Down And Under

From many angles, the whole of Australia looks like some glorious, vast theme park. So, to be the playground of the world's playground you must surely be something a bit special. You could say that, or you could say that the good citizens of Elston created a monster.

The paradox in Paradise is that they have turned it into the only spot on Australia's east coast where they block out the sun. They have pulled off the difficult trick of abolishing afternoons. There are so many high-rise hotels and apartments on the sea-front at Surfers that they form a solid wall, behind which the sun dips at around 2pm. The beach that was the original point of it all is plunged into shadow and, by four, you have to paddle out half a mile on your surf-board before you catch any rays. An hour later, the whole place is suffering from five o'clock shadow. They have killed the goose that laid the Gold Coast and a cold wind blows through the concrete canyons.

Not that anyone is too worried. Around ten million tourists come to the Coast every year, over four million of them staying overnight and the rest fleeing when the sun goes down after lunch.

What Surfers lacks in the pleasures of the natural world, it makes up for in amenities. Buildings are going up all the time to peer over the shoulders of the existing ones towards the ocean. I'm in one of them, on floor thirty-something of a block of units (see Chapter 2) so new that the staff don't yet know where the lifts are and you have to scout around for them yourself. These units set new standards of luxury for the trip, including glass-fronted bathrooms that give you a panoramic view of the whole area as you perform your ablutions or soak away the tensions of the day.

This arrangement causes concern amongst some very senior BBC staff, who wonder whether, if they can see most of Surfers Paradise whilst in the bath, it means that Surfers

Paradise can also see most of them. As so often in matters pertaining to the Corporation, one's instinctive sympathies are with the viewer.

One thing you don't see a lot of in Surfers Paradise is actual surfers. There are traces of the pioneering days of the sport in some of the older – that is pre-1980s – hotels, but most serious surfies these days head elsewhere, to edgier, trendier spots on the coast.

That leaves Surfers with the families, the hens and stags (bucks in Australian) and – menacing shimmer of strings – the Schoolies. School leavers' week in November is a newish Aussie tradition, loosely based on Spring Break in America – seven days of licensed hooning, binge drinking, drug-taking and casual sex. Surfers is a favourite destination for what is a rite of passage for parents as well as kids, because if you get them back in one piece from Schoolies, you must feel like you've done your bit. They are battening down the hatches for the invasion, the fights in the streets, the arrests – and putting up the 'Welcome Schoolies' banners. And it doesn't stop with Schoolies; there are also Toolies, older hoons who attach themselves to the merriment, and Foolies, younger kids who come along for the ride. Is it my imagination, or will there soon be Ghoolies, the troubled spirits of the casualties of years gone by?

It's one of those areas in which Australia shamelessly apes the States, rather than following the traditional blueprint from the Old Dart. You remember it: Friday – leave school; Saturday – buy first pair of long trousers; Sunday – attend chapel; Monday – start down pit or up chimney.

Another is (or are) the question of singular plurals, as in following the American aberration of saying that England is going to win the World Cup, rather than England are, or the Gold Coast Titans is going to win the Grand Final.

The Surfers Paradise headquarters of the Titans, the

Titanium Bar, is a mini-leagues club, just across the road, overlooking the Nerang River and the jetties to which the whale-watching boats tie up – whale sightings guaranteed. You can watch them come and go from a deck overhanging the boardwalk, play the pokies under life-sized action shots of Scott Prince or Preston Campbell, or dine for a laughable $10 - four quid at the rate of exchange before the pound began to plunge. For all its faults, you can live well in Surfers for little more than loose change. It has unpretentious eateries from all points of the compass – European, Asian, even South American; it caused some consternation when I returned to the unit as the sun went down one lunch-time and revealed that I had just had a Brazilian.

The Titans are the latest manifestation of top-flight rugby league in an area so full of potential players and spectators that it cries out for a truly successful club. The first attempt in 1988 was actually based over the NSW border in Tweed Heads and known as the Gold Coast-Tweed Giants – always a tricky name to chant. Tweed Heads Seagulls, whose foundation date of 1909 makes them Australia's oldest rugby league club outside Sydney, took them over and renamed them the Gold Coast Seagulls. Even with Wally Lewis as player-coach, they failed to seize the imagination and they resigned from the ARL Premiership after the 1995 season – only to re-emerge as the Gold Coast Chargers, playing in a cornea-burning strip of turquoise, purple and gold, the following year. After attempting various mergers that never quite happened, the Chargers closed down in 1998.

The game on the Gold Coast would not give up the fight, however. After a series of knock-backs, a new consortium finally got the go-ahead to try again in the 2007 season, calling themselves the Titans because that was one of the few names not tried so far. Another thing which had contributed to the various franchises' ambiguous identity was their nomadic existence at various grounds in various parts of the conurbation. They have a permanent home now in the suburb of Robina, rather a remarkable one at that, and it was there that the World Cup's most brimming poisoned chalice so far was to be allocated to the designated drinker.

Skilled Park, the naming rights having been bought by a workforce company, is designed like a smaller version of Brisbane's Suncorp Stadium – still Lang Park to me – with the innovation of a roof like a gigantic marquee. The prize for winning there, if you could call it that, was a semi-final against The Best Australian Team Ever at the Sydney Football Stadium – a slightly daunting thought if you aren't even Ireland's best-ever.

On the other hand, this was probably the best combination Fiji had put on the field to date, although I retain a soft spot for the Bati of 1995, who put an unaccountably arrogant South Africa so firmly in their place. You expect a bit of razzle-dazzle from them – you can see that on a training night at Rochdale. The surprise was how well organised they were in the pack, where they were helped by Brisbane's Ashton Sims, an extravagantly moustachioed forward who made them look like twelve Fijians and a German porn-star.

This was one night when the Irish didn't get it off Pat – Richards, that is. Fresh from best man duties at his brother's wedding, he turned out to be the worst man to be kicking for goal in a sudden-death match in the World Cup. Ireland battled all the way, but went down 30-14. They could have been satisfied with a contribution to the tournament that exceeded all reasonable expectations, but they weren't – and their captain especially wasn't.

When Scott Grix was named as Ireland's skipper for the

World Cup, I had to check first of all which Grix he was. He's the Wakefield Grix, as opposed to the injured Simon Grix of Warrington, and he turned out to be an inspired choice. He may or may not ever be a master tactician, but when it comes to leading by example he was one of the stars of the whole affair.

It was typical of him that he finished the semi-final qualifier looking as though he'd been in that shoot-out alongside Ned Kelly and hadn't made it as far as the courtroom. With a head-wound inadequately strapped-up and so battered he had to be helped into the press-conference, he summed up the Irish attitude. Surely he must feel proud of their efforts? Not a bit of it. They'd blown it and he was thoroughly pissed off. Was I interviewing a Grix or that character from the film that I saw with the grandkids – the Grinch?

Afterwards, I saw him being propped up in the corridor, still raging at the dying of the light. His Fijian counterpart, Wes Naiqama, kept his face straight when he said that they fully expected to beat Australia in the semi. It was not a night when you could fault either side for attitude.

Later that evening, I ran into someone else who was beating himself up for not winning the World Cup – Scotland's Mick Nanyn. Two days earlier, the Scots had lost their ranking game to Tonga, ending a tournament which had brought them their first-ever win at this stage and, surely, a good deal of satisfaction. Mick, a lower division points machine who had just signed his first Super League contract with Harlequins, was as one with Grix the Grinch. He was having none of this 'brave little minnows' bullshit. 'We should have done better,' he said. 'Simple as that.'

Nanyn was not even cheered up by being nominated for the World Cup's Best Dressed Player award. When the organisers were putting together their illustrated media guide, the only portrait they could find of him showed him in a bow-tie, no doubt at some end-of-season awards bash. Even after taking an airbrush to the offending neckwear, he was still in a different sartorial class from the rest of the squad. But did that cheer him up? The hell it did, but another couple of days drinking to forget on Cavill Avenue might well have done. Further down the main drag, a few of the Irish were getting into their stride in one of the resort's several 'Irish' pubs. Surfers Paradise was serving its purpose.

Ninety minutes down the coast by bone-shaking mini-bus is a very different species of Australian seaside. It was my middle daughter who told me I had to go to Byron Bay, describing it as the highlight of her own six months in Australia. Mind you, she also told me to go to the set of *Neighbours*, so I obviously only take her advice when I feel like it.

I bought my ticket from two old geezers from Malta, who had been living on the Coast for fifty years and were tanned to the colour of, well, Maltesers. Mention of the World Cup triggered some reflections on sporting strengths and weaknesses in the old and new worlds. 'England, she's-a better for-a soccer, but Australia always-a better for-a rugby league.' I can't imagine why I was talking like that, but for some reason I was. One of my new mates told me that when he was a kid in Valletta he used to collect empty bottles, cash them in and fly to England to watch the football. It's a long time ago and he couldn't remember who he used to watch, but they must have had hefty deposits on bottles and very cheap airfares in Malta in those days.

My only travelling companions were two girl back-packers from America. They were soaking wet and shivering uncontrollably, having been wrong-footed by some weather they hadn't been expecting – Ron Hill Syndrome as it is now known in Australia.

Down And Under

As luck would have it, the tune playing on what my offspring tell me is called an MP3 as we approached Byron was Nic Jones' magisterial version of a little ditty he calls *The Humpback Whale* – proof with its local references that the town's main function, although you would never guess it now, was once as a whaling station. *The Ballina Whalers*, as it should really be called, was written by a Scot named Harry Robertson, who emigrated in 1952 and worked, for the last ten years of the industry, on the whale-boats that operated out of Byron and Ballina, the next town down the coast.

Like the whale-watching, the whale-catching was made possible – and lucrative – in these parts by the humpback's migration route taking it unwisely close to this stretch of coast. If they're so intelligent, you'd think they would learn. The song includes my favourite whale-processing lyric, referring in glowing terms to the dexterity of the Aussie whalermen, who 'stripped the blubber from the whale like they're skinning kangaroos.' If they ever make an album called 'Music to Watch Whales By,' it should be side one, track one, if that's a concept that makes any sense on an MP3.

Harry Robertson died in 1995 and is one of the men of letters not commemorated at Byron Bay. As you can see through the bus windows coming into town, plenty of others are, although only because of a typically Australian confusion. The Byron after whom the passing Capt. Cook named the bay was a distinguished navigator of the day and the grandfather of the romantic poet, that 'mad, bad and dangerous to know' Lord Byron. When it came time to name the streets of the growing town, the misconception had taken root that it was called after the poetic Byron and many of them were given literary associations to match. Hence Browning, Burns, Carlyle, Cowper, Dryden, Jonson, Keats, Kipling, Marvell, Milton, Ruskin, Shelley and Wordsworth

Welcome to Oz: Australia faces New Zealand at the Sydney Football Stadium - after the opening ceremony of the thirteenth Rugby League World Cup

Tropical flavour: Jessie Joe Parker spills blood for the cause as England meet Papua New Guinea at Dairy Farmers Stadium, Townsville, North Queensland

Four Nations: Scotland, France, Ireland and Tonga make a lively start in Canberra and Parramatta

Island hopping: When Samoa met Tonga at Penrith Stadium it was one of the highlights of the entire competition. Samoa edged a blockbuster of a game 20-12.

Victoria falls: England had high hopes of success ahead of their Pool One game with Australia in Melbourne - it did not end pleasantly for Tony Smith's men

AUSTRALIA 52 ENGLAND 4

Getting serious: Fiji were one of the biggest successes of the tournament before eventually losing to favourites Australia in the semi-finals. *Below right*: The pressure got to Ricky Stuart

Major strides: Scotland and Ireland both made a big impact on events - with the Scots collecting their first ever World Cup victory after beating Fiji 18-16

Cross of St George: England's second defeat to New Zealand in a fortnight ensured that the 2008 World Cup ended in disappointment for thousands of travelling fans

Turn up for the book: Despite being given no chance at all beforehand, the World champion Kiwis stood tall to win a thrilling 2008 World Cup final at Brisbane's Suncorp Stadium

all get a jersey. If you've ever done A-level English Literature, it's like a nightmare dash around the syllabus. Not many Australians make the team-sheet, although two notable exceptions are Lawson Street, which runs along the main beach and Paterson Street, which winds inland. Neither Henry Lawson nor Banjo Paterson wrote a lot about rugby league, but in their different ways they said enough about the great split in the Australian psyche to be well worth both a detour and a place in the Byron Poets XIII.

Andrew Barton Paterson – always known as Banjo – is the man who wrote what should have been the national anthem of Australia, but when it was put to the vote *Waltzing Matilda* was inexplicably beaten by that bog-standard podium-packer *Advance, Australia Fair*. There were enough die-hards, by the way, who wanted to stick with *God Save the Queen*, to vote that sorry piece of work into the bronze medal position. Paterson, the son of another Scottish emigrant, also wrote *The Man From Snowy River* and the classic lamentation of the city-dweller who yearns for the Australian open spaces he has hardly seen, *Clancy of the Overflow*.

The poem tells of the writer trying to get in touch with Clancy, an alter-ego if there ever was one. An answer comes to his letter:

> *'Twas his shearing mate who wrote it and*
> *verbatim I will quote it:*
> *'"Clancy's gone to Queensland droving and*
> *we don't know where he are."'*
> (That same problem with is and are even
> then, you see, but they don't write them
> like that any more.)
> *'And I somehow rather fancy that I'd like to*
> *change with Clancy,*

Down And Under

*'Like to take a turn at droving where the
seasons come and go,
'While he face the round eternal of the cash-
book and the journal,
'But I doubt he'd suit the office, Clancy of the
Overflow.'*

In a sense, that dichotomy between the urban reality of the country and the myth of the outback was his only theme – and one that defined his own life.

Although often described as a 'bush' poet, Paterson lived and worked in Sydney, where he had a solicitor's practice. Henry Lawson, for one, thought that led to him over-romanticising Australian rural life, and much of his own work, like *The Drover's Wife*, is a conscious reaction to that. But Lawson's standpoint was actually very similar; that of the city-based writer conjuring up the outback. His is a bleaker vision, though: 'Through city cheats and neighbours' spite, I've come to be past carin'.'

Lawson ended his life as a celebrity drunk, reduced to begging on Circular Quay, although not, as far as I can find, to playing the didgeridoo, and is buried in Waverley Cemetery, on those cliff-tops between Bondi and Coogee. His work has not entered the national popular consciousness in the same way as Paterson's, but his name is famous enough that anyone of prominence who happens to share it, like the Australian Test seamer, Geoff Lawson, is routinely nick-named Henry.

You go down Lawson Street and past the junction with Paterson Street North to get away from the slightly tacky town of Byron Bay towards the lighthouse on Cape Byron that marks Australia's most easterly point. It's a thought to savour that this, a few minutes' walk from Keats and Shelley Streets, is as far away from England as you can get in this country. Go any further east and it's next stop Chile and the other, longer way home. From a slightly different angle, you look south along Tallow Beach – a seemingly endless stretch of sand without a building or a human being in sight.

Byron is a very different matter. The abattoirs and meat-packing works have long gone, not to mention the whaling port, leaving a town that has been re-invented by a new wave of inhabitants and visitors often bracketed as 'alternative lifestylers' or alt-lifies, to cut them down to usable Australian. That's the story, at any rate, but Byron didn't look very alternative to me, despite the recommendations of my middle daughter and of another confirmed fan of the place, the much-travelled Steve Mascord. There were plenty of washed-up rock-types there, which probably accounts for his enthusiasm, but it looked suspiciously to me like the same mix of pubs, shops and restaurants you would find in a trendified suburb like Newtown. All perfectly pleasant, but more of a little sampler of Australia than an alternative to it.

One potential difference might be that you can probably go anywhere you like in Byron without shoes, singlet or indeed anything else but board-shorts. That was certainly the case at the Railway Friendly Bar, next to the disused station. It is owned by Tom Mooney, a memorably bad-tempered winger for South Sydney and Manly in the 1970s. There were plenty of under-employed musos lying around the beer-garden waiting for the rumour of some work, some old-timers who appeared to pretty well live there, but no Tom Mooney. He was up-country, hunting or fishing or both, the Irish barmaid told me. I bet if I'd found Craig Salvatori's bed-and-breakfast it would have been the same story.

It was one of the recurring themes in the papers, on the TV and radio that the world-wide economic crisis was something going on in the rest of the world. There are exceptions, of course; if you're trying to farm in one of the areas that hasn't been getting even the meagre rainfall on which it depends then you don't need any lessons about living through hard times. But the general mood was summed up by one faintly self-congratulatory headline which read: 'Recession to Hit Australia Last.' I might be reading too much into it, but I pick up an implication there that, by the time it reaches the Lucky Country, the crisis will have had its teeth pulled elsewhere and will have lost its killer instinct. There is an alternative scenario. It is that all the ex-footballers will one day come back to their businesses at the same time, they will do the sums and the Australian recession will start. Not that I expect the Railway to contribute greatly to this collapse, because early on a weekday afternoon you have to fight your way - in a friendly, alternative manner, of course - to the bar, trying hard to remember the time of your bus, allowing for NSW and Queensland being in different time-zones at this time of year.

Before climbing on board, there is a warning of things to come. Sitting on the verandah at a fish restaurant on Lawson Street, I come across some friends who want directions to the Cape and the lighthouse. I send them on their way and five minutes later feel a slight pang of what could be guilt as the sky goes black and an apocalyptic storm drives everyone indoors and brings a tidal-wave of alternative nick-nacks, healing crystals, hair-braiding paraphernalia and henna-tattooing kits sweeping down Jonson Street, just at the time when they would have been out in the open with no available shelter.

It was sufficiently spectacular that I was seriously worried about them. I shouldn't have been, because at the other end of the beach, where they were, there wasn't a single, solitary drop. It was a sure sign that something even more unexpected than usual was happening to the weather on the east coast.

Plan A had been for England to be based on the Gold Coast during the run-up to the semi-final against New Zealand, but the hotel they had in mind for their base was no longer available. That was not a comment on their form so far, nor a closure forced by an early gust of the recession, but simply a change of ownership. Plan B was to go to Brisbane early, which meant both countries sharing training facilities at Eastern Suburbs – although not at the same time.

It's a short sprint up the Pacific Highway to Easts, a tidy little ground that is a reminder of how strong the Brisbane club competition used to be, and what a force this suburban club was within it, especially when John Lang was at the helm. Lang, a future Kangaroo coach, hooked for Australia as an Easts player and later coached the club before moving on to Sydney. Rod Morris, a member of the 1982 Invincibles, was another Easts Tiger, as were players who plied their trade successfully in England, like Paul Khan, Gavin Jones and Cavill Heugh. Even more startling to picture is that, in the days before the Brisbane Broncos, it was on grounds like Langlands Park that Wally Lewis, Mal Meninga, Gene Miles and the rest used to run around, literally at the bottom of the neighbours' back gardens.

It's perfectly fine for a training paddock, though, and England seem in good enough spirits when they arrive. The sight of them in their training kit is enough to remind the small group of Poms waiting for them how very, very badly we want them to win this semi-final. You have to try to be objective, of course, but there is any amount of enlightened self-interest pushing you in the opposite direction.

If you write about the game for a living, you would be a fool not to want the national team to do well. In fact, if you look at it that way, it's a miracle that I've been employed doing that for the last thirty years. Heaven knows, I've had little enough good news to report – and I don't want to push my luck any further. Come on, you Poms.

And yet, there's more to it than that. Rugby league is a small world. You get to know most of the prominent players on the scene to some extent or another – and to like them as people. There are exceptions, of course, but there aren't many out-and-out ratbags in rugby league; the sheer rigour and intensity of the game has a way of knocking that nonsense out of you. There are one or two lairs and hoons, but that's a different story. You would be a blind fool not to respect their courage and essential honesty – something that is hard to match in any sport but which is part of your basic kit in rugby league.

So you want them to win. You know how much work has been involved in getting every single one of them to this stage in their careers and how much it would mean to them to win a World Cup, or even – let's be realistic – get to a final. Objectivity be blowed; let's get this damned game won. I think of the wise words of a local correspondent I met in my early days covering the game. 'I'm a Batley bloke,' he said, 'writing about Batley players in a Batley team for Batley folk in the Batley paper. Neutrality be buggered.'

There was also, believe it or not – and he probably doesn't – a great reservoir of goodwill towards Tony Smith. He had been on a bit of a charm offensive before the World Cup. Not only had he said all the right things – about British-style rugby, getting the ball wide and that sort of stuff – but his team, admittedly in a couple of fairly undemanding games, had shown signs of putting that philosophy into operation. He had also told his players that there would be none of this business of treating the World Cup as a prelude to an Australian holiday. Everyone would fly back home together, because he wasn't going to be stuck on his own with the World Cup in front of the world's cameras! As a declaration of intent, you couldn't fault it. I rather liked the image of coach Smith squinting into the sunlight at the front of an open-topped bus in Trafalgar Square, or more likely in front of the George Hotel in Huddersfield, with the ticker-tape coming down in torrents and Adrian Morley, perhaps, in the forgivably dishevelled Andrew Flintoff role.

Between our brave boys' departure and the arrival of those hopeless Kiwis, there's time to explore Easts' adjoining leagues club. It's full of familiar and half-familiar faces.

You can get a cup of coffee served by Andrew Gee's wife and the photos on the wall past the inevitable pokies include a slim Shane Richardson and a Shane McNally with hair and a beard – and both of them are really called Shane, by the way. McNally of that ilk was, during his time as coach of Wakefield, responsible for passing on my favourite aphorism about the game. It referred to a lower-grade Grand Final in which he played for Easts as a teenaged up-and-comer. The match was dominated by a grizzled veteran prop playing his last game before retirement, which rather begged the question of why he was calling it a day. 'That's the trouble with rugby league,' he told the bright-eyed, curly-haired young McNally. 'By the time you learn how to play it, it's time to retire.' It's a thought originally credited, believe it or not, to the artist Titian, who is supposed to have said, towards the end of his life, that he was just starting to get the hang of the oil-painting caper. But how much more true it is of rugby league than the old cliché about what a simple game it is. If it's such a simple game, how come it's so bloody hard to play well? By the end of the week, a few people on that bus that's just pulling away from the training ground will be looking for an answer to that one.

Down And Under

Rugby league is such a cerebral game, in fact, that you should always grab any helpful supplement that comes your way. Hence the irresistible lure of a lunch of crumbed lamb's brains in Easts' bistro. The look on the face of the Press Association correspondent as I tucked into these delicacies was not one I will quickly forget. An unprecedented mixture of horror and fascination – and that from a man who has spent half a lifetime watching Great Britain/England play rugby league. I could see his point. Those breadcrumbs were a tad indigestible; the brains, on the other hand, were so fresh they were still thinking of where the next graze was coming from. They certainly did me no harm, although I did find that I tended to follow the flock that afternoon.

That sheep-track led to Kiwi training. A cheery wave from Wayne Bennett, something that must drive the Aussie press mad, because he tends to cold-shoulder them. No doubt, if he knew us better, he would have an equally low opinion of us. Still struggling at half-back and hooker, by the looks of things. Time for a chat with Manu Vatuvei about how much harder it is going to be against England this time. Against the men of mystery, the masters of timing about whom the prophet Penguin warned? Yes, of course it's going to be harder.

Some weeks later and back in England, I run into a couple of World Cup reminders. There's Damien Blanch, preparing for the new season with Wakefield and revealing a) that his Irish tattoo is on his foot and b) that his room-mate was Wayne Kerr. 'Everyone laughs when I say that, but he's a good fellah. It was all part of the togetherness we had as a team that we had no choice but to make friends with people we didn't know that well. We all did everything together as a squad, even got in trouble together. There was a curfew one night and we thought it would be best if we all broke it.'

Then there was a man whose very name is part of the Gold Coast's history, Trinity's community and marketing director and Dewsbury hooker, James Elston. He's polite enough to make a convincing fist of looking interested at being told that his is the forerunner of one of Australia's most famous and evocative place-names. It would be a simple matter for him also to change his name by deed-poll to something that would be a little more eye-catching on the Rams' team-sheet, a little meatier for the ground announcer to get his teeth into; a double-barrelled title for someone with a double-barrelled role in the game.

'And at number nine, sponsored by the West Riding Refreshment Rooms... Jimmy Surfers-Paradise!'

It worked for one Elston, it could work for another.

Ray French limbers up for commentary duties

7

Brisbane And The Taming Of Australia

Nowhere in Australia has changed as much, to my eyes, over the last thirty years as Brisbane.

As recently as the early 'eighties, it felt less like a state's capital city than a big country town. Even now, Queensland is the only state where more people live outside the metropolitan area than inside it. But Brisbane, whilst it doesn't dominate its hinterland in the way that Sydney or Melbourne do, is barely recognisable as a country town these days.

There is still a lot of 'country' about it, but it is now a big country city. The low-rise skyline of recent memory has been replaced by skyscrapers squeezed in wherever there is a gap for one. My block of units – a word I'm really getting used to - is a case in point. From 1910, it was the site of the Brisbane Stadium, a basic brick and corrugated iron structure that staged boxing, wrestling and, for a while, roller derby. That was replaced by the Festival Hall, the city's premier music venue, which amongst many others hosted the Beatles, Bob Dylan, Led Zeppelin and AC/DC, with that unfeasibly small school uniform. Now, as you walk in past a permanently harassed reception desk, there is a Wall of Fame, featuring them and hundreds of others who performed there before the hall was demolished in 2003. The new building still maintains its tenuous links with the entertainment industry in another way, because from our balcony it was hard to avoid looking straight in through the open window of the pole dancing school in the block opposite. I say 'hard to avoid' – if you grabbed the top of the railings and leaned out at an angle of forty-five degrees over the swimming pool, I'm told it was downright impossible to avoid.

Brisbane has a talent for ideas that seem really stupid but work amazingly well. Take Streets Beach, in the middle of the city on the banks of the Brisbane River, for instance. An artificial beach in a country that has half a million natural ones – where's the sense in that? And yet it has been immensely popular, both with locals and visitors.

I maintained my record of never having been there without running into Neil Fox, who not only looks about 40 years old but is burnished to a hue of which a Maltese coach operator would be proud. Neil is leading a tour group, along with Alex Murphy and Billy Boston, who must have been otherwise engaged that day. The most keenly felt absence from the ranks of the Streets Beach regulars was that of David Topliss, who had died earlier that year.

I know what the other three thought of England's World Cup performances thus far; you don't have to believe in the possibility of communicating with the departed to have a pretty shrewd idea of how Toppo would have seen it as well. Pretty much the same as one of his contemporaries, perhaps, because I couldn't help thinking of a nice touch of pre-World

Cup mischief from Brian Lockwood. Brian, a man who calls it as he sees it and, if people don't like it, so much the better, was a member of the winning side in 1972. As a speaker at a dinner, he was asked the inevitable question: 'How would they have shaped up against the present day squad?'

Well, he was the soul of discretion and diplomacy. It would be close. It could go either way. They might have the edge in fitness; we might have the edge in skill. 'Mind you,' he said with a wicked twinkle, 'we could run out of steam in the last 20. We're all in our sixties now.' It's an old joke, but still a relevant one.

Another Brisbane innovation is the twenty-four hour, city centre, open-air pub. There's one in the middle of Queen Street, the main downtown shopping mall. You would think it was a recipe for chaos, these cheerful drink dispensaries on tap at any hour of the day or night, especially in a city crawling with Kiwi cricket fans, as well as their league supporters and our own shell-shocked troops. There isn't really a Barmy Army that follows the national rugby league team around, but it does have a small Squalid Squadron who made their presence a little too obvious one night.

If the Pig and Whistle – note the absurd suggestion that it is some sort of English-style operation – has a fault it is that its toilet facilities amount to one little lock-up cabin. You have to get the key from behind the bar and, just to prevent you wandering away with it absent-mindedly, it is attached to a two-foot long ladle; call me suspicious, but I have never ordered the soup there. This was all too much of a rigmarole for a couple of our Squalids, who simply stood out in the middle of Queen Street and communed with nature in full view. It was the one moment when the whole idea no longer seemed such a brilliant breakthrough.

Brisbane is unequivocally a rugby league city. It is the fervour of the place for the game that guaranteed the success of the State of Origin concept, when the popular view in NSW was that 'mate against mate' could never quite be fair dinkum. It is where Super League was hatched – on a paddle steamer trip down the Brisbane River after Wigan had beaten the Broncos in the World Club Challenge in 1994, to be precise. The Broncos have been Australia's most successful club over the last twenty years, as well as its best-supported. Those in Queensland who opposed Brisbane's entry into what was then the Winfield Cup in 1988, on the grounds that it would kill the local competition, were right in their fears to an extent. But the Queensland Cup, in which clubs like Easts now play, is the best feeder league in the country, the best competition outside the NRL, in fact.

There has never been a question over Brisbane's willingness to support representative football and it boasts arguably the world's best rugby league stadium. Not such a bad place for a World Cup semi and final then – and all the more enjoyable for Queenslanders in that it can be interpreted as a slap in the face for Sydney.

We'd better explore the whole issue of the Queensland mentality at this stage, because Queensland is not just a few lines on a map; it truly is a state of mind. It is not a matter of blood or birth or boundaries; I know this because some of the most fervent Queenslanders I have known have actually been born and raised on the 'wrong' side of the NSW border. It's that well-known syndrome, the zeal of the convert, something which applies alike to Catholics, Communists and neo-conservatives. It's more a case of buying into a set of assumptions about what it means to be Australian – a lot more Australian, at any rate, than those cockroaches from down south. It has something to do with once being administered by New South Wales; something to do with feeling less polluted by urban life than their neighbours. At its sharp end, it produces something close to Queensland

Nationalism, the wilder shores of which were explored by the near twenty-year reign of Joh Bjelke-Petersen.

This iconic Queenslander was born in New Zealand of Danish parents, but ran the state as its Premier from 1969 to 1988. To call him a rigid, far right-wing conservative would be like saying that Chairman Mao was slightly to the left of centre. He turned Queensland into what an old colleague called 'the world's only Fascist democracy' – and he was a Queenslander and, overall I think, an admirer. Joh and Flo – his missus – were a bit of a music hall double act, but he was deadly serious about hanging onto power. His attitude to criticism is summed up by a quote that makes you wonder whether he ever considered a career in corporate public relations.

'The greatest thing that could happen in this state and this nation would be if we got rid of all the media. Then we could live in peace and tranquillity and nobody would know anything,' he once said. Small wonder that the chattering classes loathed Joh Bjelke-Petersen, but the more they and the rest of Australia scoffed and sneered at the old monster, the more Queenslanders voted for him.

State identity can express itself in a variety of ways. At stressful moments in State of Origin, the men in maroon have been lifted by the battle-cry of 'Queenslander!' More often, it reveals itself by saying nothing at all. If you conjure up a mental image of the laconic Australian, teeth clenched to keep the flies out, never using one word when none will do, that man you have created is probably a Queenslander. More specifically, it might well be Wayne Bennett.

He coached the Broncos for even longer than Joh ran Queensland and it was not an era noted for his flights of fancy in public speaking. He conducted some press conferences with the use of just three words: Yes, no and maybe – with maybe the clear favourite. In his autobiography, *The Man in the Mirror*, he reveals that his idea of a good night out is a meal with his daughters, at which not a single word is spoken. With a track record like that, it's startling news that, the day before the semi-final, Wayne wants to chat.

He wants to chat about the book. He's willing, for the benefit of an article I'm writing, to chat about Allan Langer – one of his greatest discoveries and one he claims he never thought would make it. Always keen to acknowledge being wrong, is Bennett; just like all our own leading coaches (only joking.) Most of all, he wants to chat about the World Cup; what a joy it's been and what a scandal it is that there is still a body of opinion in Australia intent on running it down.

Apart from being a committed anglophile – a legacy of his stint as a player at Huddersfield – Wayne is fiercely internationalist in his outlook. He is one Australian who can see the strategic advantages for the game in Australia getting beaten. Mind you, that's easier for him to argue now than it was when they lost under his coaching to New Zealand in the Tri-Nations in England in 2005 and he gave the slip to the waiting jackals at Brisbane Airport, on the grounds that he had nothing to say. Not like the chatterbox we find in the Kiwis' hotel this day; I wear out two pencils and a Dictaphone, but the most intriguing message is one which is never quite spelt out, but only hinted at. It is that this New Zealand side might have one big game in them that could surprise everybody.

Before that, though, they have to play England – Ouch!

A bit gratuitous, that, but that was the way they made you feel about their prospects in the run-up to the semi. Tony Smith, apparently smarting at some of the criticism of his side's efforts, goes to earth and Adrian Morley is left to do the glad-handing at the Broncos' leagues club and training ground at Redvale. I've always been impressed by the lack of fuss that characterises their facilities. It's a rough, sweaty old gym with a footy field in front of it. You would expect something flashier, but it somehow transmits the right aura: This is a place of work, not a posing parlour. Stephen Kearney is drawn out sufficiently the following day to express his disappointment at England's reluctant promotional effort.

'We've got a World Cup semi-final to sell,' he says.

And that semi, of course, is at Lang Park, now known as the Suncorp Stadium, but still The Greatest Footy Ground in the World.

For such a famous stadium, so redolent of the traditions of the game, Lang Park is surprisingly young. It was, at various times, a graveyard, a grazing meadow for goats and a rubbish tip, before it was developed as a stadium and staged its first Test in 1962. I first went there for the Brisbane Grand Final in 1981, with Artie Beetson playing his last serious game for Redcliffe, who were beaten by Mal Meninga's Souths, and I was instantly seduced by the place.

It was a rugged old joint in those days, with open hills at both ends and minimal facilities, but it reeked of atmosphere. After big games, it looked from a distance as if those hills had sprouted a record crop of dandelions, thanks to the tens of thousands of empty XXXX cans from the Castlemaine brewery next door. If anyone ever says that there is no such thing as home advantage, that a rugby field is a rugby field, they cannot have played at Lang Park against Australia, Queensland or the Broncos – who, after an aberrant exile out of town, now play there as well.

It's thoroughly modernised, of course, but still tight to the touchlines and full of the passion for the game for which it is famous. Visiting teams can find their knees turning to water before they get there; just about the time they pass the Caxton Hotel, in fact, and get ritually abused by the already tanked-up home fans. I'm like a cat on hot bricks from waking up early on match-day morning, but I think with good reason. In thirty years of covering internationals, this is the biggest game, the most important from a British point of view.

More important than a World Cup final? Yes, because if you lose that you're still World Cup finalists. More than an Ashes decider? Certainly, because if you lose that you've still lost the series 2-1 and there is no great disgrace in that. But for this game, the difference is stark. Win and you're in a World Cup final and all's well with the world, for a week at least. Your paper will be on the phone demanding reams of copy and there will probably be a bit of well-paid broadcasting to be done. Lose and your players go home – together or separately, nobody really cares – as the biggest flops ever to return to England from Down Under. Your paper denies all knowledge of you, but cuts off your expense account. The circus leaves town.

One way England kept you on your toes during the World Cup was that, although they were always pretty bad, they were by no means always the same sort of bad. Against Papua New Guinea, they were the sort of bad that comes from underestimating your opposition and scraping an undeserved win. Against Australia, they were simply out-classed to an embarrassing degree in all areas of the game. In Newcastle, they forgot how to defend.

In Brisbane, it was different again. They tried their guts out, but they found another way to lose by playing like men who had never seen a rugby ball. They might not have been very good, but, in their own way, they were rather versatile. I lost count of the number of times the ball was thrown behind the potential receiver – and not just slightly behind, yards behind. Technically, they were light-years behind. Almost despite themselves, they got within six points of the

Kiwis three times, without ever remotely suggesting that they could catch them.

One colleague was on the phone early in the second half changing his flight home and by full-time he was booked on the following day's plane. I wasn't having any of that, but it was still a stinking feeling.

And yet, in positions where sheer effort can almost be enough, we hadn't been bad. Throughout the tournament, it was hard to fault the work of Jamie Peacock, Adrian Morley and James Graham. They had done their jobs, without perhaps finding that extra ingredient of inspiration that might have lifted the whole team. In James Roby and Mickey Higham, we'd had two generally effective hookers. So the basic building-blocks for a decent performance were in place.

What went wrong, then? Well, just about everything else. The back-row would be best described as anonymous. Rob Burrow and Danny McGuire were what they are – exciting ball-runners, but not play-making half-backs. Leon Pryce wasn't really there, all his mighty form through the season evaporating when it mattered. An injury didn't help, nor might have a court case hanging over him, although a cynic could point out that it had hardly bothered him before.

Then there's the back-line. No convincing wingers, of course, but the man whose experiences and extra-mural activities really sum up the whole trip is Keith Senior. As an international rugby league player, Keith has been a credit to his trade, not least because he has always made himself available when others have chosen not to, playing willingly through injuries to which others would have succumbed. He has been a major figure in Test football, but if the game in Britain was as healthy as we are told it is, he would surely have been superseded by now by a younger model and perhaps re-routed into a last hurrah in the pack. But no, the fact is that, along with a spasmodic Martin Gleeson, he is still the best we've got, so there he remains.

His trip and its aftermath turned out to be more memorable for reasons unconnected with playing. First, he was the victim – if victim is the right word – of a bonk-and-tell sting in the News of the Screws. The most surprising aspect of that was that an ageing centre in the world's third-best rugby league team merited the attention. You notice I've scrupulously avoided the term 'column inches' there.

Then, after going home, he made the debatable decision to sell his World Cup medal on ebay. I can see why it didn't mean much to him; every player got one, so it was nothing special. I haven't worn my free England shirt very often, for that matter. For one thing, it has a nasty if unintentional hint of the National Front about it; for another, it arouses nothing but bad memories. But if you want to get rid of your medal, give it away quietly to a boy in a wheelchair, like Matt King did when he was a non-playing squad member in the Tri-Nations a couple of years earlier. Take it to Spurn Point and skim it into the North Sea, I'd suggest, but don't try to get a measly few quid for it on ebay, even if you then give the money to charity. If you do, you stir up the whole vexed issue of spirit in the England camp. He might be proving me wrong as I write this by putting it up for sale on the Irish equivalent of ebay – galwaybay? – but I somehow doubt whether Wayne Kerr has flogged his medal.

Nor, I reckon, will many Fijians. The following day, they got their inevitable come-uppance from Australia in the other semi-final in Sydney, but if there is such a thing as a good 52-0 defeat, then this was it. Fiji played with great passion and determination, best typified by a tackle from Jarryd Hayne that almost cut Darren Lockyer in two, but Australia produced plenty of the brilliant rugby that made them such obvious favourites for the Cup.

In the New Year, I ran into Mike Ratu (Snr) at Leigh for their pre-season friendly against Oldham. 'You know,' he said, 'I was still proud.' Fijians everywhere in the world were entitled to be proud. By all accounts, the World Cup made a huge impact on the islands. The most impressive fact was that you could not buy a satellite dish anywhere in Fiji, such was the demand. And I'll bet you still can't buy a World Cup medal at Suva market, except possibly Keith Senior's.

Back in Brisbane, it's a question of what to do now. You have to feel for the British fans, who at least thought they would have a final to look forward to. As usual, I rely on the rather banal piece of advice I always offer on occasions such as these: Don't let the rugby spoil the trip. It's not going to spoil mine. In fact, the easing of the work-load for the following week opens up all sorts of possibilities. Brisbane isn't a bad place to be under-employed.

The first distraction is on the Monday night and involves a return to Lang Park/Suncorp for the International Federation's Player of the Year Awards. It's a little difficult to find the way in and, as we try one of the wrong ways, an imposing figure is coming back towards us. 'No offence fellahs,' he says. 'But if I can't get in that way, I don't think you can.' It's Mal Meninga and he's probably got a point.

It always causes an outrage at these events if a non-Australian wins anything, so there is no doubt about the headline of the night: James Graham is the world's best prop. It's the last act of a marvellous season for Saints' Scouse scourge, who has won just about all the individual awards going. The Aussies have certainly warmed to him, with the result that there are no riots in the streets about him being preferred to the Australian front-rowers, Steven Price and the Suva-born Petero Civoniceva. In fact, the strongest complaint about his selection comes from Graham himself, but that's Scousers for you – always whinging. Jammer actually describes himself as 'embarrassed' to be named ahead of two such seasoned campaigners, but he is a popular winner. It says something about the standard he has set in Super League, however, that for all the favourable impression he has created in Australia, we actually expected even more from him.

What we didn't expect, what even Ron Hill didn't expect, was what was about to hit us. You never see a picture of Brisbane without the sun shining; I think they were made illegal during the Bjelke-Petersen Premiership. The reality is rather more complex. One afternoon, a cloud the size of your fist settled above the swimming pool. Within a couple of minutes, the whole sky was black, the rain was lashing down and the thunder was echoing down the city streets. The only people unconcerned about it all were the pole-dancers across the street, who carried on their practical studies with diligent seriousness, lit up intermittently by the lightning. It was bad enough in the city, but a lot worse on the northern outskirts, where people were losing their roofs, their garages and, in some cases, their entire homes. 'The worst storm in thirty-five years,' they said – and to think, if we'd gone home early we would have missed it.

The World Cup finalists did their bit with a morale-boosting visit to the secondary school at The Gap, the area worst affected by the deluge. The damage didn't look too bad at first, until you look up into the higher branches of the eucalypts and spot the aluminium panels that were once somebody's roof. The neighbourhood is literally up a gum tree.

In fact, my taxi driver reckons that the gum trees are part of the problem. People like them in their yards, because they look the part, but when the big winds come, down they crash onto your house. The ones that aren't secretly rotten enough at the core to fall stick around to catch some of the flying debris. The trip has its desired effect, especially when the Kiwis get on stage at morning assembly and perform the best haka of the entire tournament. Attempts to persuade the Australians to respond with the Macarena are unsuccessful, but I think England's morris dancing would have gone down well.

I collar Steve Price and ask him about Graham's comments. His response is the most gentlemanly you could imagine, even from a practitioner of that most civilised of trades in the front row. He's just being modest and humble, Price says, he's a fantastic forward and he deserves to be rated number one. It's heart-warming stuff, this mutual admiration between old prop and young prop; I think it has the makings of a Walt Disney movie in it somewhere. It does make me think back, though, to a story that Barrie McDermott, Ireland's assistant coach in the tournament, once told me. As a wild, young newcomer, Barrie played for the first time against Kevin Ward, who was pretty much state-of-the-art at the time. Bazza did his best to batter him and wasn't too fussy how he did it. After the match, Ward took him on one side, congratulated him on his performance, told him he had a big future in the game and offered him advice if he ever needed it. The next time he played against him, Barrie's team-mates asked him what was wrong.

'Why aren't you smashing him like last time? Get out there and get him belted.'

'But he's such a nice bloke....'

'Aha,' they all went, 'You've been 'old-manned'.'

We won't find out for a while, but I'm not totally convinced that James Graham hasn't been 'old-manned' by Steven Price.

The gathering at The Gap also gave me the opportunity to

run the rule over the New Zealand forward, Greg Eastwood, who I think has a different sort of rort on the go. If there's one thing I love it's a player you can't possibly confuse with anyone else. It can be something as mundane as a silly hairstyle, although that can be rather ephemeral. In fact, when Danny Brough goes to the barbers, he usually tells them that he wants it ephemeral down the sides. It's best if the instant recognition rests on a player just looking and playing differently from any other player. One of my favourites, Danny Sculthorpe, falls into that category, although he has the daft hair as well, just to make sure he has all the bases covered. Eorl Crabtree is another, with his combination of the physique of Hulk Hogan, the physog of Gerard Depardieu and the hairdresser of Sean Long. I've also acquired a new favourite in Stefan Ratchford, who looks like one of the more gormless young characters in *Coronation Street* and moves and plays in an utterly distinctive way. You would never mistake Paul Cooke for any of his team-mates and I'll bet Brian Bevan never had a try credited to someone else in error.

You'll never see another one like Greg Eastwood either. Or you won't in Super League or the NRL. You might in the North-West Counties or the Pennine League, because, to put it politely, the lad looks like a pub player. With his ample arse, broad beam, chubby cheeks and any number of additional alliterations, Eastwood just doesn't look the part. He even plays with his socks rolled down. If he goes to his family home for five minutes, he puts on a couple of pounds. He somehow managed once to put on weight during a match – which sounds impossible to me.

That's the set-up. The sting is that he's a hundred times more mobile and agile than he looks, with fast feet below those saggy socks. He ambles towards you, lulling you into a false sense of security, then someone waves a burger from the back of the stand and – whoosh – off he goes. He's going to be tremendous fun and, if he ever gets there, will never be confused with anyone at Leeds, except perhaps a couple of lads propping up the bar in the Supporters' Club. He's already been responsible for one classic commentary moment: 'And it's Eastwood tackled by Westwood.' It makes you wonder what Ike Southward would have made of it all.

He might have appreciated the honesty of the answer Greg gave when I asked him why he was leaving all this and coming to Leeds at the age of 21.

'For the money,' he said. No mention of new challenges, new horizons, seeing the world; this lad really is something special, but I had to let him go and build his ark.

When the second wave of the week's biblical deluge hit the city, I was on my way to the Jubilee Hotel in Fortitude Valley, a journalists' haunt opposite the old Exhibition Grounds, where Great Britain fought and won the Battle of Brisbane in 1958 – the one where Alan Prescott played on with a broken arm. 'The Worst Storm in Brisbane for 48 Hours,' the TV declares. The streets are awash, with chairs and tables floating past and, when I shelter under a concrete verandah, I can't help noticing that it's buckling and bubbling.

What is it about Rugby League World Cups and rain? I thought I had seen it get as bad as it gets during the 2000 tournament, when the roof gave up the ghost at Twickenham and a waterfall crashed straight into the man from the *News of the World*'s lap-top. The road from Gloucester to Wrexham was almost washed away and then it really started to rain – especially that night at Llanelli. Look at pictures of our brave boys who won the World Cups in 1954 and 1972 and there's plenty of mud on them as well. Are we really cursed for breaking up the happy home that was rugby before 1895? It makes you wonder, all the more so when they're baling out and mopping up in the waterlogged ground-floor bar at the Joob.

The Jubilee is about half-way to Brisbane's most celebrated pub – The Breakfast Creek Hotel, so called because the creek, in the days of ox-carts, was as far as you could get from Brisbane by breakfast time. The Brekky Creek is a big, rambling building, with an even bigger, rambling beer-garden, much of it given over to the chomping upon what are justifiably claimed to be the finest steaks in Queensland – which is the same in these parts as saying the best in the world. The pub also has a claim to inventing Mad Monday – the footballers' full day on the piss with which they let down their hair after a long, hard season, or before it, if you're Salford. There are rival claims to the invention, most of them in Castleford, but at the Brekky Creek you can sit out in the sun, eat a steak every six hours and stay there until Mad Monday turns into Tranquil Tuesday.

The other major distinction of the place is that it is the only pub in Australia where they serve XXXX from a little wooden barrel on the bar, into which they hammer a tap amidst much foaming of beer. Not everyone is impressed. 'It tastes a bit.....woody,' says the man from PA.

Time, gentlemen, please for a brief digression into the national scandal that is Australian beer. If there is a commodity anywhere in the world that is more hype and less substance, I have yet to find it.

You might have got the impression so far that it has never passed my lips, but that is not quite the case. On a hot day, I've been known to knock over a few bog-standard cold ones when it would be rude not to, but that's what it is – bog standard. It might induce fierce brand loyalties, but I'd defy anyone in a blindfolded test to distinguish between any of the major brands at the temperature of minus ten degrees at which they are served. Given that they taste pretty much the same, people develop weird preferences; some will only drink stubbies, some only long-necks, in their slightly slimmer bottles. And then there's all that business about different glass sizes; that's why people get thirsty – from working out all this stuff.

Australian beer is at its best when it goes so far out into left-field that it leaves the ball-park. Barrels on the bar fall into that area, so you have to drink it even if it's like chewing splinters, but so is brewing a deliberately cloudy range of beers that taste of something at room temperature, cellar temperature or even ice-cold. Hats off to Coopers of Adelaide, a national life-saver if ever there was one. When I first lived in Sydney, there was only one pub that served it, so I would go up there at least once a week and come back to Bondi with a cardboard box-full of clanking pint bottles. Happy days.

In the week leading up to the World Cup final, we sub-let the spare bed vacated by a colleague doing a runner to the editor of a distinguished rugby league magazine, whose original digs were flooded-out. No, we didn't want any money, we told him, he could just provide the beer for the working session in the apartment after the game. How much beer would that be, he asked. Whatever you think, I told him. He came back with eighteen pint bottles of Coopers Pale Ale. Do you sometimes think that someone has been studying your *modus operandi*?

The relaxed week before the final provided a perfect opportunity for a little exploring. Ron went up to the humorously-named Sunshine Coast to see his old mate, Darryl Van der Velde, but, as was to be expected, the Brisbane weather followed him. Some headed for the Glass House Mountains, where they couldn't see the front end of their cars for the solid wall of rain. I opted for a place from which I thought I might see Brisbane from a slightly different angle.

The earliest settlement in Moreton Bay, which sweeps to the north and south of Brisbane, was the penal colony at Redcliffe, which took the baddest convicts from Botany Bay, as the soft, southern Sydney area was still known. Redcliffe proved too inhospitable even for convicts and the colony was shifted to the banks of the Brisbane River, whilst Moreton Bay was thrown open to settlers. Cleveland, at the southern end of the bay and half an hour on the train from Brisbane, still has buildings from the mid-nineteenth century, which makes it ancient in Australian terms. It has Queensland's oldest pub and – contain your excitement here – its oldest banyan tree. Actually, I'd recommend the banyan; it's an absolute monster and, at night, it's illuminated from within by eerie coloured lights.

Cleveland was intended to be part of a pincer movement to cut Brisbane out of the deal, by acting as the port for Ipswich, the rival settlement a little further inland. It never quite happened, partly because its jetty burned down at an inconvenient time, leaving Cleveland as a quiet backwater. That placid atmosphere was enhanced, I thought when I was there, by what I took to be sign-posts to even more peaceful places. Who wouldn't fancy a lazy weekend on Refuge Island, or a leisurely couple of days at Slow Point? It was rather a shame to discover that they were merely traffic directions.

Cleveland is actually a good bit busier than it was, thanks to the redevelopment in the 'eighties of a mangrove swamp into a housing estate of canals and cul-de-sacs called Raby Bay. It must have seemed like a good idea at the time; it would be opposed now as a crime against bio-diversity.

The township also has a sizable bowling club and it was there that I saw a truly shocking thing. There, at the sort of institution that has sustained all traditional Australia's obsession with being kitted-out correctly, there was a sign reading: 'First Tuesday of the Month! Barefoot Bowls!' Has it come to this? It's certainly to be hoped so; I liked the idea of all the old sticklers rolling over in their graves at such an heretical idea, but perhaps that's just my bias.

In any event, there was to be no more bowling that night, barefoot or fully shod, because the clouds were scudding in off Moreton Bay and Stradbroke Island and it was starting to hose it down again. 'The Worst Storm in Brisbane Today,' claimed the papers, TV and radio stations, although that was a news angle that was starting to lose its impact. This was around the time, though, that the theory started to take hold that New Zealand's only chance of winning, or even keeping it close in the World Cup final lay in the prospect of even worse weather than we had seen so far. We scanned the forecasts with delight; they predicted the worst storms since Capt. Cook cruised up these coasts. There was hope yet.

The decision had already been made, of course. Almost to a man (and a woman) England supporters who had been swearing never to watch a game again after the semi-final debacle were all going to be honorary Kiwis for the day of the final. I met Australians who were profoundly irritated by this, but I tried gently to explain that it was inevitable. Poms and Kiwis have much in common, but the main thing is that they are not Australians; in a situation like this, that is quite enough to cement an alliance.

Besides, we get on well with New Zealanders. It's hardly a scientific survey, but every Kiwi who has ever come to my own humble club with his boots under his arm looking for a game has been a good bloke, willing to muck in and give it his best shot, on and off the pitch; I can't say that about every itinerant Aussie, because one or two of them have been prize pricks.

There's also an affinity that you feel when you go to their country, but it's a pleasingly exotic affinity. You see the modest scale of the place, the hills and farms and think: 'Ah yes, all very familiar, in a wrong-end-of-the-earth type of way,' but then you spot a terrain of boiling mud, a hundred-foot geyser or a glacier encroaching on the High Street and you realise you aren't in Parbold at all.

I had the opportunity to practice being a Kiwi at the cricket at the Gabba. The Brisbane Cricket Ground at Woollongabba – to give its full name, which nobody does – hosted rugby league Tests between 1909 and 1957, whenever they were not being played at the Ekka, or Exhibition Grounds. Now, apart from Queensland and Australian cricket, it hosts the Brisbane Lions AFL team.

I'm there thanks to a members' pass summoned up by an expatriate Pom I bumped into on Magnetic Island. We must have been in the posh seats, because on the other side of me was a recently retired representative of the Australian diplomatic service. We chatted about the World Cup and got onto the subject of Papua New Guinea. No, he hadn't ever been there and nor would he, after what he had heard about it. He then proceeded to tell me a story, the truth of which I cannot vouch for. Apparently, a senior member of an overseas legation made the mistake of sacking his locally-employed driver. One night, the driver's mates and relatives came over the security fence, dragged him out, tied him to a tree '....and buggered him. Repeatedly. Poor fellah went doollaly. Never the same again.' New Zealand are being treated equally roughly by Australia at The Gabba, without any recourse to underarm bowling, and, worse still, the sun is shining.

Later that day, the eve of the final, there is a Men of League fund-raiser to be negotiated. Plenty of funds are raised, thanks to Brisbanians' willingness to pay thousands of dollars for framed shirts commemorating the greats of the city's club competition over the years. Some of them are there, like Ned Kelly – the front-rower from Ipswich, not the bushranger – who tells a few tales about his first tour to Britain, facing the likes of Billy Boston. 'I was shit-scared, to tell you the truth,' he says, rather implausibly. 'And I don't think I was the only one.' There is no such admission from Barry Muir, still the angry little man he was when he played scrum-half for Queensland and Australia.

The centre of attention, however, just as he has been since he was a schoolboy prodigy in both codes of rugby, is Wally Lewis.

If Sir Don Bradman and Ned Kelly – the bushranger rather than the front-rower – have a claim to being the most famous Australians, then Wally carries a distinction that counts for more around these parts: The Greatest Living Queenslander. Not that everyone likes him; there are plenty of people who will tell you what an arrogant egocentric he was in his playing days. What no-one will dispute is that he was probably the greatest big-game player the code has seen. He still carries that aura around with him, along with the title, which he frankly dislikes, of 'The Emperor of Lang Park' – where his statue stands in front of the stadium. Someone told me that they had seen him go calling on the Socceroos in his role as Channel 9's sports presenter and they stopped training to gawk at him. It was whilst working for 9 a couple of years ago that it became obvious that all was not well and he eventually revealed that he was suffering from epilepsy and had brain surgery to relieve the symptoms. Perhaps not surprisingly, the whole experience has mellowed him considerably and he is back at work on a warm tide of goodwill.

Wally Lewis was one of those players who transcended rugby league, in the sense that you didn't need to know much about the game to see that he was very special. Take the case of a friend of mine at home.

I don't think Ian would even call himself a rugby league fan, but ever since he saw Wally Lewis throw a few of his uncanny passes on the 1986 tour he has been obsessed with him. Once, when I admitted to being inadvertently responsible for Wally being kicked out of his coach's box at Tweed Heads to make space for press overspill, he didn't speak to me for two years. Every time I see him now, he bombards me with questions in the mistaken belief that I have some sort of inside track to the great man. It's 'What's Wally up to?' and 'How's Wally?' as well as the inevitable 'Where's Wally?' Now I'm sitting two tables away from him and I know what must be done.

It's an unwritten rule of journalism that you don't ask for autographs; it establishes the wrong sort of relationship. I have made the odd exception, though: Bob Dylan; Mohammed Ali; the surviving members of the inaugural Rugby League Hall of Fame – Gus Risman, Brian Bevan, Alex Murphy and Billy Boston – in 1988; Ryan Giggs (for my lad). Now, as the giant screens show grainy old footage of matches he admits he can barely remember, I'm about to add Wally to that select list, because I couldn't face Ian again at the cricket club if I didn't. On the way, I give myself a little pep-talk. Don't mention his health problems, don't go on about the passage of time, don't say it's for your mate.

When I reach the front of the queue, I blurt out: 'It's for Ian at the cricket club. Great to see you looking so well. Don't know who that young bloke running around on that screen is, though.' Wally Lewis writes: 'To Ian. Good Luck!' He signs his name carefully and gives me a sidelong look of inexpressible weariness. At least I didn't call him the Emperor of Lang Park; the next time, I might try him with the Sultan of Suncorp.

The following morning the sun is out again and the approaching horrors are officially downgraded to a Storm in a Tea-Cup. You can get 7-1 against a New Zealand victory, now that the elements have decided that they are not going to aid the cause. Those might sound like ridiculous, even insulting odds in a two-horse race, but on a dry track who in their right mind would back against Australia? Full credit to our speccies, though; they have got over their disappointment at England's wretched displays and have thrown themselves into the project of being Kiwis for the day. By kick-off time, some of them will probably believe that they are Kiwis, born and bred in the Shaky Isles.

In the morning, there's a steady stream of Poms stocking up on those distinguished, unmucked-about with New Zealand shirts at the Canterbury shop in the Queen Street Mall. Also in the store is the Kiwi stand-off, Benji Marshall, who shouldn't really need to buy one. There's a lot of back-slapping and hand-shaking and I'm hoping they're a bit careful with him, because Benji is one of the frailer-looking players in the game and has an injury record that makes you wince every time he gets a whack. New Zealand have got as far as they have largely because he has held together, but there's no sense in pushing your luck.

Both Benji and his well-wishers are to play an important part in an unforgettable evening of rugby league. Looking back on it now, it was a match full of contradictions, with Australia often living up to their own publicity.

First, they fronted up to the haka with linked arms and an icy stare, which is an improvement on trying to ignore it, but probably not as good as retaliating with morris dancing. Then they scored two tries – both set up by the marvellous Billy Slater. He was already just about my favourite player in the game before the World Cup. There's something irresistible about his permanent optimism and willingness to chance his arm. I didn't see Clive Churchill, but there have been some great Australian full-backs since him: Graham Eadie, Greg Brentnall with the Invincibles, Garry Jack, Darren Lockyer, when he played that position, the now forgotten Anthony Minichiello. I rate Slater ahead of any of them, but I think one of the reasons for that is that he is always likely to give you a chance. Whenever I see him play, I think of a song performed by Kenny Rogers – not usually one of my favourites – called *The Gambler*.

> *'You've got to know when to hold 'em,*
> *know when to fold 'em,*
> *'Know when to walk away*
> *and know when to run...'*

It was actually written by another, less well-known country singer named Doug Schlitz and it is pretty much interchangeable with the government's responsible gambling campaign. Beer mats in pubs and leagues clubs carry messages like 'Don't chase your losses' and 'Be man enough to walk away.' No doubt it's good advice, but you rather hope it will never get through to the free spirit that is Billy Slater.

Australia hardly made a mistake in the first half and would have been 16-0 up and in the clear if Ashley Klein had not referred Lockyer's effort to Steve Ganson, who ruled that he had clearly lost the ball. That was the end of the easy video referee's decisions. Instead of 16-0, Jeremy Smith's powerful try made it just 10-6 after 23 minutes.

The rest of the match, as nobody who was there will need reminding, hung on three decisions, all of which went against Australia.

First the Kiwis got the benefit of one of those lost balls that could be either a knock-on or a strip. You can look at replays forever and still not be sure. On balance, Ganson probably makes the right call and Jerome Ropati's try stands. The Kiwis are leading and their massed ranks of adopted fans sense that something remarkable might be happening. Voices from the M62 corridor are singing 'Kiwi Til I Die' or 'Momma, Momma, We're All Kiwis Now' or, most woundingly to the hosts, 'You're Just a Big Country Town in Queensland.' Stephen Kearney reckoned he could detect the distinctive vowel sounds of Hull, where he used to play, and that the sheer volume eventually helped to get his troops over the finishing line. But so did one or two other things.

Australia scored a brilliant team try to lead at the break. It was one of those moments that made you think 'Damn! They're just going to play like that for a few minutes and they'll be out of sight.' But back came the Kiwis to lead again – and then it was time for The Gambler to over-play his hand.

I have a feeling this is going to be a famous passage of play for a long, long time. Slater does outstandingly well to field a difficult kick near his own corner flag. So far, so good, but then he thinks that, rather doing the boring, predictable thing and just taking the tackle, he might just be able to sneak outside the defence for a potentially devastating counter-attack. The trouble is that there isn't quite enough room. He is being driven into touch, giving him his second chance to fold his cards. But no, he's still trying to make something out of the situation. He lobs the ball infield, where it drops gently into the hands of Benji Marshall for a gift try. Billy doesn't even look all that upset; he's had a punt, he's done what comes naturally and it hasn't come off. That's the way it goes.

Ironically, a more pedestrian full-back might have done the safe, conventional thing and Australia might have won the World Cup. As game-losing errors go, he gets precious little criticism for it. Ricky Stuart says he wouldn't ever want him to change and the whole country seems to agree. Australia is a nation of gamblers and it understands.

Besides, their team comes back with a Greg Inglis try that is another of the game's dazzling moments and is still in with a chance until the third pivotal decision and, to my mind, the most contentious.

Nathan Fien, another of the Kiwis' surprise successes on the night, kicked through and there was no doubt that a panicky Joel Monaghan flattened Lance Hohaia as he chased the ball's parabola. But would he have got there to claim the ball and touch it down cleanly under pressure? Steve Ganson thought so, awarding a penalty try and proving again that, whether you think he's right or wrong, there is no denying his courage.

Plenty of good judges thought he was right; I was in the other camp, because I thought at the time that Billy Slater might get there first – although anything could have happened after that, of course. The debate over the ruling exposed a bit of an urban myth. The Laws of the Game do not say that the attacking side needs to be set to score definitely, certainly or beyond reasonable doubt, although many of us thought they did until we checked.

What they actually say is this: 'The referee may award a penalty try if, in his opinion, a try would have been scored but for the unfair play of the defending team.' It's not a rule that has changed recently, either. A 1968 rule-book I have on my shelves phrases it in exactly the same way. On the face of it, that makes it far easier to award a penalty try than is often supposed. But hang on a minute, let's have a look at that word 'would'. Not could or should or might have. I couldn't be sure he would have, although I might have been sure that he should have. Not quite good enough; a penalty and a sin-binning would have been about right, although, like all surrogate New Zealanders, I was happy enough that St. Steve the Brave went the way he did.

The Kiwis got a late clincher through Adam Blair, who, like Smith and Sam Rapira, turned out to be a far better forward than you would have guessed, unless you had been particularly diligent in your Setanta viewing the previous season. All you could hear was a chorus of thousands of Poms looking on the bright side of life. The Kiwis had sneaked down the blind side and Graeme Bradley had been right all along – apart from picking the wrong team to stage the ambush.

I look for Wayne Bennett, thinking that, under the circumstances, his celebrations might be fairly discrete and he might even be a little difficult to locate. Not a bit of it. He's there in the thick of the rejoicing, fists clenched and grinning, loving every moment of it. He knows that the Kiwis – his Kiwis, to a considerable degree – have saved the World Cup. That trophy, which has been destined for Australia from day one, is handed over to Nathan Cayless, by the Queensland Premier, Anna Bligh, who gets in trouble with some sartorial critics for wearing jeans.

I don't think there was any truth in the rumour that she had a ball-gown and tiara she was waiting to change into when Australia achieved their expected landslide. I would like to believe, however, that in one corner of Lang Park, a few pseudo-Kiwis were singing a little ditty that had Aussie fans completely bemused. 'Dressed up in a minute,' it went, to the familiar, all-purpose strains of *Guantanamera*. 'She's getting dressed up in a minute...

'Dressed up in a minute. She's getting dressed up in a minute.'

Sheltering from the storm in Brisbane

8

The Darling Downs, The Granite Belt And The Reclaiming Of Australia

Australia don't lose many rugby league matches that matter and they aren't terribly good at it.

Oh, they can cope with the odd isolated defeat by us poor old Poms, like Sydney in 1988 and Melbourne in 1992, and be quite magnanimous about it. But, as we have seen, when they lost the 2005 Tri-Nations final to the Kiwis, even as convinced an internationalist as Wayne Bennett dodged the national soul-searching by doing a runner as soon as his return flight home hit the Brisbane tarmac. They were never going to take the loss of a World Cup final very well.

Sure enough, the Australians went into a collective sulk, brushing – Oz-speak for giving the brush-off to – people they had known all their careers, excluding outsiders and refusing interviews. It was a different story in the Kiwi rooms. They eventually formed a circle for some player-only business, but only after they had celebrated with all and sundry, with anyone who happened to be passing.

Darren Lockyer managed to be reasonably gracious at the formal press-conference, but Ricky Stuart was clearly talking through clenched teeth, or talking as clearly as you can through clenched teeth. The whole structure of the tournament had worked against his side, it seemed. It was no preparation for a World Cup final to have had gentle run-outs against Fiji, PNG, England and, er, New Zealand. They were, in that familiar Australian phrase, under-done. I thought he might fancy a pop at the video ref, but no luck. His aim, as we were soon to find out, was to be concentrated elsewhere.

It was the following morning when Ricky met Ashley and told him exactly what he thought of his contribution to the final. It was a public outburst which no doubt made him feel better at the time, but which ultimately cost him his job. It also completed a tournament in which there was far too much talk about referees.

Apart from Stuart's tirade, England were too eager to use the officials as an alibi. Yes, there are differences of interpretation between the two hemispheres. But here's the shock news; there are differences within the hemispheres too and always have been. Part of the art of playing rugby league, one of those things you learn just before retirement, is the need to assess that day's referee, how he looks at the game, what he will tolerate and what he won't, and play accordingly. It was ever thus.

And those happy, harmonious times in the past when all referees had exactly the same ideas and interpretations, when were those precisely? We must have blinked and missed them. To tell players that they are the victims of some sinister new development is to give them excuses for failure. The same goes for those who keep telling our best players how exhausted they are. Okay, it's a long season and a uniquely demanding game, but it doesn't make it any easier to keep being told how knackered you are.

I'm knackered too, but in our different ways, we all have to keep going. Mascord is agitating for a Mad Monday at the Breakfast Creek. The snag is that we will all have gone our separate ways by then, so we settle for a Stupid Sunday instead, with steaks, schooners off the wood and a steadily expanding circle of passing Poms. There is a rumour that the Kiwis are going to be there, but they too are taking off in all directions, with only part of the squad arriving in Auckland with the Cup. That's one thing we would have been a lot better at – had we won the damn thing.

By Brekky Creek standards, it's only a Slightly Silly Sunday, but it does kick-on – another essential Australian term for your phrase-book. The club to which it kicks-on is a little history lesson on Brisbane rugby league. Past Brothers – originally known (are you still out there, Ron?) as Merthyr - used to be a force in the local comp and far beyond. In 1967, they had three players in the Kangaroo tour squad, including Peter 'Pedro' Gallagher, who captained them at White City, when Reg Gasnier and Johnny Raper were injured. There is a life-sized statue of Gallagher in the foyer. At least, they describe it as life-sized; if he was really as big as this, not to mention made of bronze, it's a miracle that anyone ever stopped him.

The Brothers clubs are something of a network across Australia. If you've been educated by the notoriously severe and militantly sports-minded Christian Brothers, you tend to play for the Past Brothers club in your home-town, otherwise they give you a good thrashing for old times' sake. If you later gravitate to the big city, or the big country town, you play for Brisbane Brothers. That was what Steve Ricketts did when he lobbed up from Lismore, on the wrong side of the NSW border. Now he lives in a house roughly on the 20 metre line of what used to be their pitch. I've explained to Steve, the long-serving and unnervingly dedicated rugby league writer on the *Brisbane Courier Mail*, how very dangerous this is. On the Indian graveyard principle, anything built on the former home of a rugby league club is hexed. Housing estates built on the site of former grounds like Watersheddings and Station Road, are places of misery, with statistics for marital breakdown, mental disturbance and home repossession which are off the graph. It is a negative equity of the soul and it is the way the unquiet buried spirits of rugby league get their own back.

A man with a rare sense of the history of the game, Steve admits to wrestling with some doubts before deciding to rent there. In the end, it was just too tempting. From his back garden, he can picture himself, just a couple of houses away, scoring that try in 1978, or whenever it was. He even has – get this – his own key for a gate in the fence at the end of his cul-de-sac that leads directly onto the leagues club's car-park. Talk about living the dream.

Brothers dropped out of the Brisbane comp because of financial problems in 1998 and now exist only as a junior club playing a little way up the road. By the time of their demise, though, their leagues club had enjoyed a second lease of life as the home of the South Queensland Crushers – one of the clubs created by the ARL's ill-fated pre-Super League expansion. I'll never forget – but will probably never fully remember either - that weekend, when a plane-load of us were transported around the four inaugural games in Auckland, Perth, Townsville and, last but not least, Brisbane, where Mike Ford and the late St. John Ellis lent a British flavour to the Crushers team that lost to the Canberra Raiders.

The Darling Downs, The Granite Belt
And The Reclaiming Of Australia

On the face of it, South Queensland had a few things going for them. For one, they were based at Lang Park, with the Broncos way out of town at the QEII/ANZ Stadium. For another, Brisbane was surely big enough to sustain two clubs. Caught up in the vicious political in-fighting of the Super League wars, they lasted just three seasons. The fence around what was once their leagues club and the gate leading to Steve Ricketts' Secret Garden, those have lasted a bit longer.

Turn left at Pedro Gallagher's statue and you are in the domain of Mark Meskell. He was a no-frills prop who was pretty close to ever-present in the Barrow team that finished fourteenth out of sixteen in the First Division in 1986-7. I remember him vaguely and might have interviewed him at some stage of his stay. On his return to Australia, he played a bit of first grade for Western Suburbs and in the reserves for the Broncos in their inaugural season of 1988. His high-water mark, without a doubt, was his year with the Shipbuilders, as he still fondly calls them. He is now the chef in the club's bistro and my apologies to anyone who was waiting longer than usual for their steak or pasta that night, because his anecdotes took priority over his barbecue and hob.

His best one concerned the night he turned up for training and was greeted like a long-lost brother by an Australian, but one who was a complete stranger, on the opposite side of the changing room.

'Mesky! Me old pal! How'ya going, mate?'

He leapt across the room, took Meskell in a bear-hug and whispered in his ear: 'The name's Al. You've known me all your life and I'm the best fucking player you've ever seen.'

Al got his contract, played one game, as far as I can make out, and the fate of English rugby league was sealed. That is to say that a pattern of recruitment was established that was to distort the relationship between the game in the two countries for many years; the back-packer syndrome, under which just about any itinerant Australian who looked the part could get a game in Britain. Al's spiritual successor must be Dave Armitstead, literally a back-packer, who was National League 2 Player of the Year with Barrow in 2008 and then moved to Leigh after being shown the door at Craven Park. Asked at the National Leagues' end-of-season dinner whether promotion with Barrow would be a challenge, he was able to answer: 'It will be for them, mate. I've been given the bullet.' As he basks in the glory of the Leigh Sporting Village, he should, despite that little set-back, say a little thank-you for the pioneering work of Al and his contemporaries.

Fittingly, I hear this story on the night when I'm organising my own back-pack for a little foray I've been planning. Grief and adversity affect people in differing ways. Some people who had come to Australia primarily to watch England had been on their way home whilst our brave boys were still standing behind their sticks looking fed-up in the semi-final. It has the opposite effect on me. I feel that, in order to balance things up a little, I ought to stay a bit longer and do some exploring.

'You're going walkabout, aren't you?' people asked and I suppose that I was, in the sense that white Australians often use the word 'walkabout' when talking about black Australians and their mysterious comings and goings. I was wandering off aimlessly, leaving any responsibilities behind for a while, abandoning my lap-top, packing my back-pack, waltzing my Matilda. The only question was where I should do it and what rugby league connections I could hook into.

I'd had a few ideas, all of which I'd had to reject for one

reason or another. There was a long-standing ambition to get to Tasmania, the original Van Diemens Land, which just sounds like a marvellous place, with its condensed pattern of rolling countryside, miniature towns and fierce wilderness. Tassie – no prizes for getting that one – used to be the only state in Australia with no rugby league. That is no longer the case, thanks largely to the work of a real rarity, a woman chief executive named Sue MacGibbon, who has now stepped down, leaving a modest four-team competition in and around Hobart. Sounds like my sort of thing, but it's an awfully long detour when your flight home leaves out of Brisbane.

Then there's Darwin, another place I've always wanted to see, although preferably not during the hot, wet season. There is plenty of development work going on at the Top End, much of it done by Duncan MacGillivray, the former Wakefield forward with the most Scottish name in their World Cup squad, but who is actually a Northern Territorian.

What about Perth? Plenty going on there, but it would feel like being half-way home. I've also been there before, on that junket in 1995, and it seemed then like an empty film-set waiting for the actors and the extras to arrive. The Queensland coast is also out of the equation, given that this first week of freedom co-incides neatly with Schoolies, that festival of under-aged excess for which Surfers was bracing itself when I was there. Once upon a time, that would have been an attraction; now, somehow, I think not.

So, what does that leave? The obvious solution is an incursion into a slice of inland Queensland I hadn't experienced before. But it needs to be narrowed down a lot more than that; Queensland is a big place – more than three times the size of France. Fortunately, I have a tiny dot on this big map already in mind – Leyburn on the Darling Downs.

There are a few reasons for heading there as a starting point, but mainly the fact that it's the home-town of a bit of a hero of mine – Shane Webcke, the thinking man's prop. Not only is Webcke one of the best-ever in the position, he also cuts across all the stereotypes about thick front-rowers. He's a deep thinker himself and a voracious reader, as well as the type of bloke who's interested in his surroundings. Best of all, he has bought the run-down old Royal Hotel in Leyburn, which could well have been on its way to a slow death, and restored it to its former glories. He won't be there, of course, because he'll be presenting the sports news on Channel 7 in Brisbane, in direct opposition to Wally Lewis, but that just shows that he respects one of the great traditions of Australian business, whereby the boss is never in.

My admiration for Webcke as one of the toughest, most determined players I've ever seen is in direct proportion to the weight of the book about him I've just bought. His volume in the series *Icons of Australian Sport* is the heaviest rugby league book I've ever acquired, beating even *The Lions of Swinton*, which I've been using for the last few years to press wild flowers and wedge the kitchen door open, it being the size of the Greater London telephone directory. Webcke's tome, a lavish production based on the scrapbooks kept by his mother and wife, makes that feel as light as a feather. It is not, therefore, the obvious choice as light reading for someone lugging his back-pack around Queensland. It was reduced from $79.99 to $19.99, though, and it can be left in safe custody in Brisbane, holding down a few items of furniture, just in case the typhoons return.

Webcke's mentor, Wayne Bennett, isn't expecting much from him in later life; just, according to his foreword to the

174

mighty tome, the possibility of becoming State Premier or running the game of rugby league. No pressure there, then. Wayne also has an opinion on where I should go walkabout.

'Go to Killarney,' he says, referring to another small town on the Darling Downs, rather than in the West of Ireland. 'Beautiful place. Very quiet.'

Coming from him, that is high praise indeed and not to be lightly ignored.

Taking in Warwick and Stanthorpe – home to the best-named country club in Australia - as well and then sneaking over the frontier to Tenterfield in NSW should kill a few days stone dead. As an itinerary, it's not going to get the leading tour companies panicking, but its sheer aimlessness should be relaxing. Other routes might attempt to show you the big picture; this book now sets out to shine a dim light on irrelevant Australia.

The great thing about the country is that, once you get a few miles away from the cities of the coast, it is basically empty. There's a sprinkling of communities, alright, but, compared to the spaces in between, they are negligible. Stand anywhere on the edge of Australia and look out to sea and you can feel the great spread of nothingness behind you. It's part of the feeling of breadth and freedom that Australia gives you. You could leave the Brisbane conurbation and travel west to Perth and not see a person or a building, if you picked your route well enough. Australians are not cramped for space and it shows. It shows in the country bloke's squinting gaze aimed somewhere beyond the horizon. It shows in the way you start to sprawl when you stand or sit, knowing you aren't competing for elbow-room with anyone else.

You don't have to get very far from the city before country Australia starts to assert itself in its own, quietly insistent fashion. In rugby league terms, it does this in a very specific way – by laying its rightful claim to names often associated with Brisbane.

To outsiders, Allan Langer, the Walters brothers and our old mate, Ned Kelly, can be bracketed together as Brisbane players. But they are nothing of the sort; they are all from Ipswich, the one-time rival now almost enveloped by it. Ipswich is the first staging-post on the road west and must have something in the water that breeds hookers – Steve and Kerrod Walters, as well as Kelly, have all played in that position for Australia. It being the centenary of the game in their country, there was a good deal of picking of Teams of the Century going on. Spare a thought for Steve Walters, one of the funniest blokes in the game, but the target of plenty of ribbing from others over his non-selection. 'No, I'm not in the Australian Team of the Century. I'm not in the Queensland Team of the Century,' he said. 'I'm not even in the flamin' Ipswich Team of the Century.' Not that it's any disgrace when the choice, in each case, is Ned Kelly.

Straight on from Ipswich is Toowoomba, a rugby league hotbed whose representative side glories in the name of The Clydesdales and which, at some points over the last hundred years, has been a match for Brisbane and even Sydney. Toowoomba, still a town of under 100,000, once supplied an entire Australian Test pack and, over the course of two years in the mid-'twenties, beat England, New Zealand, New South Wales, Brisbane....and Ipswich.

We're veering off to the left, though, down the Cunningham Highway, across the Great Dividing Range and through the back door onto the Darling Downs, named after a governor of New South Wales, and where, I note with some satisfaction from my *Lonely Planet*, 'there is not much to go out of your way for.' Excellent.

Despite that brusque dismissal, every small town in Australia is famous for something. If there was a town that was famous for nothing, it would soon be sufficiently renowned on the strength of that for it to be an attraction in itself.

Not that Allora has that problem. It has an embarrassment of choice of claims to fame. It is the sunflower capital of Australia, the hometown of P.L.Travers, the author of *Mary Poppins*, the birthplace of Wayne Bennett and the place where Shane Webcke learned his junior footy, as did Rohan Hancock, the Celtic Crusader Tony Duggan and that most convincing bushranger lookalike, Kirk Reynoldson. Actually, they all learned half their footy there, because Allora merged with the Clifton team up the road long ago, to form the Allora-Clifton Wattles. I can't vouch for Clifton, but Allora is as picturebook-perfect as anywhere Mary Bloody Poppins floated off to on her accursed umbrella. There are laurels around the doors and verandas of the wooden houses and scarecrows (to protect the sunflowers) in the gardens. Every house has a chimney (chim, chim, chiroo) because it gets chilly around here.

Further out into the back-blocks is the even smaller town of Leyburn. In fact, Leyburn makes Allora look like Mexico City; it must have been quite exciting for the young Webcke to go playing his footy in such a metropolis. Mind you, Leyburn is busy one weekend of the year, when the Vintage Motor Sprints take over and plough up several of its otherwise empty fields. And they have built a new row of motel cottages on the main drag, just about doubling its population on a good night. Across the road at the Royal, there is no Webcke, but then we knew that. The joint is being run by a forthright lady called Wendy, who comes from Julia Creek, way up in the north near Mt. Isa. She doesn't think much of Leyburn, which she regards as little better than a gentrified suburb of Brisbane. For one thing, compared with Julia Creek's year-round forty degrees, it's too damn cold – and that applies to the temperament of the place as well as the temperature, she reckons.

'They're a weird bunch here,' she says. 'You have a fight with someone and they don't speak to you for six months. Up at the Creek, you'd knock seven colours of shit out of each other and be best mates next day.' Maybe Shane has made the Royal a little too civilised, although I imagine it still gets a bit lively during race weekend, when competitors and spectators alike tend to sleep where they fall down.

After I get home, I hear about Webcke doing an extraordinary thing, pulling the plug on the autobiography he had written, with the help of Ian Heads, on the eve of publication, because he feared it was too hard on the Broncos, who had since taken him onto the coaching staff. A day later, he re-inserted the plug and let it go ahead, only to later resign at the Broncos anyway. With footwork like that, is it any wonder that he was harder to tackle than the average, head-down prop and that there is talk of a career in politics? Or perhaps he'd taken delivery of his new book from the printers, weighed his options and decided it was just too lightweight by comparison with his earlier works. Can't wait to read the offending section and wondering whether I should threaten to have this one pulped.

A slightly eccentric route to Warwick takes us past Wayne Bennett's new homestead, on a good block of land well back from the highway. I'm half expecting to spot him out on his veranda, waving a cricket bat at us invitingly, but I know really that he's already getting his teeth into his new job at St. George-Illawarra. How can he leave Warwick, a place famous for so many things that it almost needs a separate book of its own? Just to skim the surface, it is renowned for its roses, its rodeos, for throwing eggs at Prime Ministers and for the invention of a special sort of singlet worn by sheep-shearers. If that isn't enough to justify its place on the map, I don't know what would be.

The roses and the rodeo are a potentially poignant combination, crying out for an as yet unwritten Country 'n' Western song about a tragic riding accident. Both were out of season when I was there, but the story of Billy Hughes and the egg is timeless. Even after about a century of Bob Menzies, the aquatic Harold Holt and the Governer-General's sacking of Gough Whitlam, Billy Hughes remains Australia's most famous Prime Minister – at least until Shane Webcke is ready for the job. It was during the First World War that he came to Warwick to speak in favour of conscription and a disgruntled listener caught him squarely with his missile – yolk and white all over his dress-coat. Hughes wanted the perpetrator arrested, but the local constable, whose sympathies seem to have been with the egg-thrower, claimed he had no jurisdiction – and that led to Australia adopting a federal police force.

Then there was Jackie Howe, a record-breaking shearer from these parts, who once clipped three hundred and twenty-one sheep in a day by hand and was allegedly the first to wear a sleeveless vest for the job. That garment is now known as a Jackie Howe and he has a memorial in Warwick. Better than that, he has a motel named after him at the top of Palmerin Street. It has quite a swanky dining room, so it's quite possible that you could be turned away from the Jackie Howe for wearing a Jackie Howe.

Anna Bligh, the Queensland Premier until Webcke moves in, is a Warwick girl and she is in the clear sartorially. No-one in her home-town will hear a word against her

World Cup final jeans. As far as Warwick is concerned, she was pretty dressed up.

I'm not stopping at the Jackie Howe, but across the street at the Horse and Jockey, largely because it was once owned by a genuine rugby league legend. Harry Bath isn't there, of course, but he has a cast-iron excuse, having died earlier in the year. A brilliant second-row with Balmain, Warrington and St. George, he is credited with taking Australian techniques to England and English techniques to Australia. He was equally successful as a coach and he had the biggest ears in rugby league.

'It's pretty quiet here,' the manageress tells me apologetically. 'The town shuts down at eight in the week.'

'Excellent. Can we persuade it to shut down at seven?'

Actually, I need a bit of time, because I'm off to see the Warwick Cowboys.

When the town's two clubs, Collegians and Eastern Suburbs, decided to merge, they wisely opted to draw inspiration from the rodeos rather than the roses. They were glad, all the same, to get away from the Warwick Showgrounds that rugby league used to share with the bare-back riders. It wasn't unusual, as well as the horse manure, to find the odd horse-shoe on the pitch down there. They now play just down the hill from the Horse and Jockey and the Jackie Howe, on the banks of the Condamine River, which occasionally freshens up the playing surface by flooding all over it. On the opposite side of the water, Easts and Collegians, still separate as junior clubs, have their pitches.

At the Cowboys, Peter Coote, who used to play on the wing for them alongside Wayne Bennett, has a lovingly tended museum and archive of everything pertaining to rugby league in Warwick. I liked the stories about the local police sergeant, Eddie Brosnan, who, when he coached the side, used to give young miscreants the choice between a court appearance and trying their hands at rugby league. They got some of their best players that way. Eddie was Wayne's uncle; it's all a bit close-knit around here.

As the stalwarts of the game in Warwick gather for a chin-wag, you can tell you're among real rugby league people when they say things like: 'Y'know, I reckon it was good for rugby league, the Kiwis winning the final' and 'Shame the Poms didn't front up, though.' The goodwill even extends to local boy Bennett's involvement in Australia's downfall. 'Although my wife calls him a turncoat,' says Peter. 'Mind you, she's still dirty on him because he was the one who introduced us.'

It hadn't all been merry banter for the Cowboys in 2008. In January, three of their young players died in a smash on the Cunningham Highway, on their way back from a 21st party – something that understandably knocked the guts out of the club for a time. They were planning a candlelit concert in their memory on the first anniversary of their deaths.

I like Warwick, although the locals are right when they boast that there isn't an awful lot to do there. The Shire Council, however, does put out a little pamphlet of suggested walks. One takes you along the Condamine; another to the disused railway station where Billy Hughes was egged and the crumbling O'Mahoney's Hotel across the road; and one around the red sandstone buildings of the town centre. Set into the wall of the Town Hall is a memorial to the local rugby league players who died in the First World War – no less than nineteen of them.

I'd already been there once when Gerard Walsh took me back. I'd called in to see Gerard at the *Warwick Daily News*, surely one of the more astonishing survivors among small-town daily papers, where he is rugby league writer, sports editor and probably a few more things as well. He was just back from almost winning an award for his coverage of the Cowboys' tragedy – a job that must have been made harder by his knowing all the families personally – and I wanted to get some idea from him of the importance of rugby league in a community like this.

Like a good journo, however, he turned the interview around, so that he was quizzing me about what I was doing there, what I thought of the place and why England were so crap in the World Cup. He wanted a picture of me, looking serious at the War Memorial and the story was a page lead a couple of days later. You don't have to do very much to qualify as news in Warwick.

One of my new mates at the Cowboys had kindly offered to take me to Killarney and that, after what I'd been told about the place, was an irresistible proposition. It involved going through Yangan, home village of Mick Madsen, one of the great Australian forwards of the 'twenties and 'thirties, although he was actually born ten miles down the road at Tannymorel. Madsen played for the Brothers club in Toowoomba and was recalled to the Aussie side as a late selection for the third Test against the Lions in Sydney in 1936, becoming the first player to be flown to a Test. It's a modernist claim to fame that feels strangely at odds with the handful of wooden shacks he called home. They played him out of position at hooker, by the way, and it was a bit of a disaster.

Killarney, you will not be surprised to learn, was settled by Irish immigrants in the late nineteenth century and was named for its supposed resemblance to the West Coast of Ireland. It used to have its own version of the Lakes of Killarney, until the farmer whose land they occupied decided to drain them and use them to grow crops. Cabbages, by the looks of them, as we went past.

It hasn't always been quiet in Killarney. I was just a couple of days away from the fortieth anniversary of the night in 1968 when a typhoon hit the town and flattened two hundred and thirteen of its two hundred and forty houses, as well as most of its public buildings. Ron Hill is not thought to have been in the vicinity. Only one person was killed, although the toll would have been far worse if it had not been the school's prize-giving evening, in one of the town's theatres, which was one of the few buildings not to collapse. Apart from that one unfortunate girl, it's an almost biblical story of deliverance.

At the top end of town is its biggest employer, the abattoir. But for a couple of inconvenient details, I could go in and meet the owner, the former Test forward, Rohan Hancock, once again. The snag is that he has just sold the place for millions and I know for a fact that he's in Brisbane. That's where he was when he told me about selling the slaughterhouse and he was not in any hurry to get back home. Hancock spent his playing career in Killarney, Warwick and Toowoomba and he can be seen as a milestone in Australian rugby league. Of all the scores of players who represented the Kangaroos from country clubs, he was the last when he toured with the 1982 Invincibles – the last of a dying breed, as you might put it in his line of business. When I asked him in Brisbane whether he thought of himself as the final link in that distinguished chain, he gave a convincing impression of a man who had never considered such a question. 'Suppose I might be,' he said.

Above Killarney, there are a couple of natural features that re-arrange your perceptions of just where you are in relation to Australia's centre of gravity. Brown's Falls,

Dagg's Falls and Queen Mary Falls come tumbling out of springs in the Great Dividing Range. Although you're only a couple of hours as the crow flies from Brisbane, this ice-cold, frothing water is not destined for the east coast. It will feed into the Murray-Darling system and eventually emerge into the ocean near Adelaide. Like Ricky Stuart's vocabulary when he saw Ashley Klein the previous Sunday, we are beyond the watershed.

The local rugby league team is called the Killarney Cutters, a reference to the old timber business – mainly cedar – in the area. That's not a bad name, but the christening of country clubs is not something Australia does as well as it should.

The main reason for that is the glamour of Sydney. Country towns all over the country follow in the city's footsteps by having their Magpies, Tigers and Roosters. It's only when they look beyond those that they get creative. There are a couple of good examples in this part of the world; the Goondiwindi Boars and the Freestone Crowbars both seem to carry eloquent suggestions of the way they are likely to play. I have a couple of favourites in New South Wales, as well; the Parkes Spacemen and Russell Crowe's club – not just because of all the boozing and brawling we've done together – the Orara Valley Axemen.

But the best of the lot have to be the Stanthorpe Gremlins. How the hell did they come to be called that? Anything to do with the film? There is a tenuous rugby league connection there, because Shaun Edwards' nickname, Gizmo, is a reference to a creature in *Gremlins* – a movie which was all the go when he was establishing himself in the Wigan first team in 1984. I've found that, the closer you get to Stanthorpe, the more adamant people are that there's a really fascinating story behind it, without ever quite being able to recall what it is. Thus it is that I'm on a Crisp Coach to Stanthorpe, to go to Crisp Real Estate and meet a man called Crisp, who will hopefully be able to give me some crisp answers.

Strictly speaking, Stanthorpe isn't in the Southern Downs; it's part of a separate sub-section of South Queensland known as the Granite Belt.

It's off the main routes, but vaguely well-known for its cold, its apples (crisp ones, naturally) and its wine. Of the three, it is most fiercely proud of its low temperatures. There are jealous pretenders to its title of Coldest Place in Queensland, but it plans to rout them by erecting a giant granite thermometer by the causeway over Quart Pot Creek.

This is the Australian way. If you want to show the world that you are the top place for something, you stick up a huge version of it – be it pineapple, sheep or minus degrees – on Main Street and the argument is over. There is undeniably a nip in the air as I disembark and find that Crisp Real Estate, run by a cousin of the bus-firm boss, is just down the street.

Norm Crisp has been a player and just about everything else for Stanthorpe Rugby League Club and he is the man who knows where the body of its former identity is buried. The club didn't used to have a nickname as such, but they wore a big red apple on their left breast and were informally known as The Apple-munchers or The Apple-crunchers. In the early 'seventies, they brought in a hard-bitten type of coach who had played first grade in Sydney and he said: 'I'm not coaching any team called the flamin' Apples!' He went into the sports store across the street – it's still there – and asked them what they had in the way of badges that looked fierce. He leafed through a catalogue until he found a truculent little sprite with pointy ears and cried 'Eureka' – and the Gremlins they have been ever since.

It's a convincing story, but unfortunately Norm has no picture of the Gremlin handy to show me. That's why I have to come back with one of the more unusual requests an estate agent's receptionist might have to field: 'Has the boss left a picture of a Gremlin for me?' He has and I can see why it became the public, very ill-tempered face of the club. It looks a little like Ricky Ponting when he cops a really poor lbw decision, or the BBC's David Oates on a very bad day.

The Gremlins have a long tradition of fielding itinerant English players, including a couple of high-profile recruits in Ian Sherratt and Dean Busby. Sherratt, a prop forward with Oldham and, rather more briefly, Wigan, is still warmly remembered for his marauding play in these borderlands. 'We just followed him around and we had a great season,' recalls Norm. "He had his twenty-first here and everyone finished up in the Creek.'

I promise to pass on fraternal greetings to any former Gremlins I come across in the Old Dart. Statistically, there is a better chance of running into those who have been employed in the area's fruit harvests. That's the difference. Our back-packers pick peaches; theirs play in the back-row for Barrow.

The other suppliers of seasonal work and income are the wineries. The Granite Belt's wine industry is a bit like England's – absolutely tiny, but, on the quiet, pretty good. I forget what insignificant percentage of Australia's wine the Granite Belt produces – and I have unaccountably lost my notes from a day's intensive research – but it had a decimal point and lots of noughts in it. That modest scale means that you might not be able to taste everything on one trip, but you can see just about the entire crop, stacked up in various barns and sampling rooms. Not that everyone appreciates it. Our driver, one of a long-established Italian family of winemakers, recalls picking up one visitor who was carrying that indispensable item of Australian summer kit – an esky. Very thorough, thought Mario, he obviously wants to keep all the wine he's going to buy at the optimum temperature. Not a bit of it; the esky was full of chilled beer, which he proceeded to drink all day without ever getting out of the mini-bus. 'Little fellow with a broken nose, he was. Something to do with football. Name of Tommy Raudonikis.'

As a league icon with a foot in both states – born in the scrum-half nursery of Wagga Wagga, played most of his rugby in Sydney with Wests and Newtown, but a long-time Queensland resident – Tommy would appreciate Stanthorpe's situation near the NSW boundary. They and teams like Killarney and the Texas Terriers – snappy name, but you can't really go wrong with a town named Texas – play in a Border League with the New South Welshmen of Tenterfield. It's there that I'm bound, but there are a couple of must-see destinations on the way.

Bald Rock has what might, on first hearing, sound like an underwhelming sales pitch – The Second-Biggest Rock in Australia! – until you remember that the biggest is Ayers Rock. The granite outcrop is a mere fraction of Uluru's awesome bulk, but whereas the custodians of the Red Centre now discourage you from climbing up it, Bald Rock has helpful footprints painted on it to show you the way. It used to be a bit like that at Ayers Rock. When I went there, the best part of thirty years ago, I climbed up it, walked along it, ran around it, watched the sun rise from it, saw the sun set upon it. 'You've done everything to that rock,' my girlfriend at the time said, 'except shag it.'

Near Bald Rock is little hidey-hole associated with a man who has a claim to be Australia's number two bushranger – after you-know-who. That might be pitching it a little high, because Aussies have never stopped singing about Jack Donohue – 'The Wild Colonial Boy' – and Ben Hall has had his own TV series. But Captain Thunderbolt has the most evocative name – better than his original one of Frederick Wordsworth Ward – and is definitely up there in the first division.

He was involved in eighty hold-ups and robberies, all in this border country, until he was killed in a shoot-out at Uralla. Or was he? There were reports of sightings after his supposed death and there is a theory that it was his similar-looking half-brother who was shot. It really should be his likeness on the badge of Border Bushrangers, as the local representative side is called, but, wouldn't you know it, it's unmistakably that other bloke, who never even picked a pocket around these parts, looking smug in his trademark armour and helmet. For Captain Thunderbolt, it's not so much a case of 'Damn you, Ned Flanders!' as 'Damn you, Ned Kelly!'

Tenterfield, home of the Tigers in the groundbreaking cross-Border competition, has done more than its share for national unity. It has a claim to being The Birthplace of the Nation, because it was there in 1889 that Sir Henry Parkes made the key speech of the successful campaign for the federation of the original, separate colonies to create Australia as we know it.

It is also a small town with a particularly insistent sound-track. Peter Allen, the singer-songwriter who was born there, wrote mainstream hits like *Don't Cry Out Loud* for Elkie Brooks and *I Honestly Love You* for Olivia Newton-John. He was also responsible for *Tenterfield Saddler*, written as a tribute to his grandfather, who was exactly that and whose shop still stands on a side-street like a sort of shrine. Allen was also married for a time to Liza Minnelli, before he became one of the first Australians in the public eye - even before Ian Roberts - to come out as obviously gay, although marrying Liza Minnelli should have been a clue. The song of his you are perhaps most likely to be able to hum is the one that Qantas used in its advertising for years. 'I've been to cities that never close down,' it begins. 'From New York, to Rio, to old London town.' Actually, Qantas took out Rio, to which they did not fly, and replaced it with Rome, to which they did, but which doesn't scan.

'But no matter how far and how wide I may roam,

'I still call Australia home.'

Depending on your taste, it's an unofficial national anthem, tapping into the exile's longing for his home turf, or an appalling dollop of schmaltz, churned out by someone who had been living in California for years. It doesn't do to be too picky about these things. 'I still call Australia my second home,' doesn't scan either, but it was probably true for Peter Allen, who died of AIDS in 1992, and the longer I spend there, the more true it is for me as well.

A few days later, back in Brisbane, I'm in Tommy Raudonikis' local. I think he used to own all or part of it, but details are sketchy. I ask the barmaid if he's around and, without checking anywhere but my corner of the pub, she is adamant that he isn't. How can she be sure he isn't lurking somewhere in what is a pretty crowded establishment? 'Because you're sat on his stool and he would have shifted ya by now,' she said.

Australia....I think I always will call it some sort of home.

The image that just won't go away

9

Aftermatch: Hong Kong
And The Replaying Of Australia

I turn on the giant plasma television in my mate Niall's twenty-ninth floor flat off Wing Fung Street and something vaguely familiar looms up to meet me. Is it....can it be? It is! Scotland versus France in Canberra from almost six weeks earlier.

Later that night, I notice that the girlie bars of Wanchai, the seamy end of town where I used to live, are not quite doing their normal brisk trade. Sure enough, the reason is obvious when I get back to base and turn on the telly: Ireland versus Fiji on the Gold Coast. A couple of days later, I have it fathomed. Now Sports 6, one of a dozen sports channels, is showing an endless loop of the entire World Cup. Some of it feels so old by this stage that it would sit better on a station called Then Sports, but three nights running, I come in, turn on the TV and find myself watching England losing to New Zealand again. It's like Chinese water torture.

Sustained by a Tsingtao beer or two, I make myself watch it all. It confirms one or two impressions; England still have four different ways of losing a game, none of them much to do with refereeing interpretations or the length of the domestic season, and the penalty try still looks dodgy. The ball still hits the wings refreshingly often when other teams are playing and some of the finishing is superb. It's handsomely entertaining – especially by comparison with the turgid Bledisloe Cup game between Australia and New Zealand that they staged in Hong Kong a few weeks earlier – but I can't help wondering who else, in all the teeming apartment blocks that allow mine just one slim oblong of harbour view and that from the roof, might possibly be watching it.

But then, the entire issue of television and the World Cup was a bit of a puzzle. The whole tournament was essentially designed to suit Channel 9, who had a terror of one-sided games. Union watchers will cluck indulgently about brave little Malawi or whoever; but it seems that leaguies are liable to riot in the streets, or, even worse, turn off their tellies, if every game is not fair dinkum. Hence the odd structure of the qualifying groups and Papua New Guinea's Mission Impossible. Having got what they wanted, however, 9 showed precious little interest in maximising the value of what they had paid for by screening matches live. You could have kept up with the tournament better sitting at home in Bolton, or probably in Hong Kong as well.

I was musing on such matters on the top deck of the tram to Kennedy Town, unavoidably soaking up the Chinglish business signs that have survived re-integration with the mainland. In amongst all the ones that claim to be Splendid or Marvellous, there is the endearingly modest So-So Hair Salon; there's the Dear Restaurant, the Minute Hotel – named, I like to think, for the size of its rooms rather than for your preferred length of stay; didn't that say the Ah Fook Pork Co? And there's the Creative Accountancy Company, whose specialised services I might well be requiring if I am to pass all this off as book research for tax purposes.

Hong Kong, I can hear the Revenue's investigators sneering, not many rugby league connections there. Well, you might be surprised. When Super League's 'global vision' was first unveiled, where did the shiny-suited revolutionaries promise that the masses would be spellbound by the game? Hong Kong, of course. Where is the World Club Challenge, or possibly a fourth State of Origin, going as soon as we can iron out the details? Why, Hong Kong. It's the final frontier.

And then there was that incident when I ran into the entire Warrington board of the time, staggering out of a Kowloon dive called Ned Kelly's Last Stand – yes, him again. Needless to say, we all staggered back in. This last time, I was in the bar ghetto of Lan Kwai Fong – a completely new invention since I lived out there – one night in the Newtown shirt I wear with such pride. 'The Jets, eh?' said one of the numerous Australian expats in the joint. 'What do you know about Tommy Raudonikis? And why were England so crap in the World Cup?'

'I know he's not in his pub,' I was able to tell him. As for Part B of the question – not a clue.

I did precious little to further the rugby league cause in the two years I lived and worked in Hong Kong, apart from managing to get the story of Fulham's birth onto the front page of the *South China Morning Post*. I even confess to playing rugby union for Kowloon; indeed, that was a condition of my board and lodging in a Government flat on Boundary Street. Strictly speaking, that probably made me a professional, a decade or two before that mortal sin became all fine and dandy in union. I left the club a season before another down-at-heel itinerant arrived – the future St. Helens chairman, Eamonn McManus. So don't tell me there are no rugby league loose ends to be tied up in Hong Kong. There's almost certainly a book in it; *XIII Woks*, perhaps, or *XIII Wontons*? It was partly because of that obscure non-connection with Saints' taipan, however, that I chose to spend my last afternoon in Hong Kong watching the worst rugby I've ever seen in my life.

I knew what to expect and I didn't mind. I'd had a perfect week. I'd walked the ridge known as the Dragon's Back to the seaside village of Shek O; watched the sun set from The Peak; caught ferries to Lantau and Lamma, where I ate seafood on the waterfront. There were a dozen restaurants bidding for my valuable custom at that quiet time of the day, each trying to make me a better offer than the rest. Full marks to the young lad who weighed up his target so accurately. 'Big bottle of beer,' he said, cutting unerringly to the chase. 'Ten dollars only.'

They appeared to be waiting for me as well at the 3-6-9 Shanghai Restaurant in Wanchai, although I hadn't been near the place for twelve years. They can't get many round-eyes in there these days. I'd gone on the Star Ferry, the old Central terminal for which is now half a mile inland, to eat dim-sum in Tsim Sha Tsui. I'd run the gauntlet of bars in Lan Kwai Fong. I'd been on the jetfoil to Macau, where the lost dollars of the Cantonese – the only people on earth who love a punt more than the Australians – have built a gilded city which overlays the decayingly picturesque one the Portuguese left behind. I'd spent Happy Hour with old journo mates who had somehow survived thirty-odd years of working and drinking in Hong Kong and were still complaining about the same old things.

I'd seen New Zealand beat England four more times. I'd packed a lot into seven days.

Aftermatch: Hong Kong And The Replaying Of Australia

I'd a bit of previous as well with Stanley Fort, once the headquarters of the British Army when Hong Kong was still a colony. I'd played rugby there – of a sort – once against the Gurkhas, who might not be very big or rugby-savvy, but my oath, are they persistent. It is also there that I was once arrested for the illegal possession of ammunition, but that's a different story.

Since the hand-over to China, the Fort has been HQ to the People's Liberation Army and very much off-limits. There is one exception to this. One day a year, the old symbol of imperial power at play reverts to type. The San Miguel-swigging, rugby-playing expat community reclaim the pitch for one Sunday afternoon to stage the Professions Sevens, just as though nothing had changed. If you wondered why the negotiations for the hand-over to the Chinese dragged on a bit, this could be your answer. 'Alright, you take Hong Kong Island, Kowloon and the New Territories,' Chris Patten must have told them. 'But we still want Stanley Fort rugby pitch for our Sevens one Sunday afternoon every December.'

Thus it is that a convoy of taxis winds down from Stanley Market, past the stereotypically impassive guards and on towards the world's most unlikely rugby ground. Once through the gates, there are few Chinese faces and nobody else in a North Queensland Cowboys shirt.

As a willowy winger for the Hong Kong and Shanghai Bank, Eamonn McManus should have been in his element in the Professions Sevens, but then again anybody who could catch a ball should do pretty well. It is not wonderful rugby – did I hear cries of 'No change there then?' – but the Guinness is chilled, the burgers are sizzling and there is champagne on ice in the corporate marquees. And nobody wants to know what the hell happened to England in the World Cup. Have these people not been tuning into Now

Sports 6? I buy Eamonn a programme so that he can wallow in a little Sevens nostalgia and head for the airport.

If anything Hong Kong seems a little more liveable than when I attempted it. A shade less sharp-elbowed, perhaps. Fractionally more polite and considerate, although still furiously entrepreneurial; as if the Cantonese had just been waiting quietly for the clumsy, incompetent colonialist capitalists to sling their hook, so that they could get on with making some serious money. And things work. At downtown stations on the Mass Transit Railway, you can check in for your flight and not see your luggage again until Manchester. That is a boon and a blessing for anyone carrying a 20lb book about Shane Webcke, but don't try it at Wigan Wallgate.

Back home, admittedly a week or two after everybody else, there is an eerie silence. The official attitude to the World Cup is reminiscent of the episode of *Fawlty Towers* with the Germans, where Basil – that's Fawlty, not Millward – keeps hissing 'Don't mention the War. Don't mention the War.'

The inquest into what went wrong is scheduled for March; in March, it is moved back to April, by which time, it seemed to be hoped, we would all have forgotten about it. The best expression of the collective amnesia that I heard came from the Castleford coach, Terry Matterson. 'The World Cup's over, Dave,' he said. 'Don't torment yourself. It's gone. Let it go.' I was trying, honestly I was, but it wasn't that easy, not when everyone you bump into says: 'Oh, you're back, are you? What the hell went on over there?'

Even Ian at the cricket club, when he had finished misting-up at the sight of Wally Lewis' signature, wanted to know. So did the postman, the milkman and the bloke who collects old clothes for the charity shop – and that's just the interrogation on the doorstep.

Further afield, the questioning became more insistent and you're not Tony Smith; you can't just say 'no comment' or that you're not doing interviews that day. Down at Bolton Mets, you have to reassure a few badly confused outside backs that, yes, a sliding defence is supposed to slide and that doing otherwise is as bad an idea in the North-West Counties Division Four as it is in a World Cup.

And then there was Tony Smith, suggesting in the course of a friendly and sympathetic TV interview that the British media coverage of his team's efforts should have been 'more patriotic' and that some of his players had been affected by the criticism of their efforts. No player has yet echoed that claim; indeed, it's hard to imagine anyone in the world's toughest team sport ever being caught saying: 'That paragraph in the *Daily Express* really put me off my game.' The closest was Paul Sykes claiming to have been made a scapegoat for a collective failure – and he isn't entirely wrong about that. Other interesting retrospective observations came from Keith Senior, Leon Pryce and James Graham, all of whom admitted that there had been a gulf between the Leeds and Saints players in the squad. Adrian Morley, speaking from the neutral territory of Warrington, thought otherwise.

But what really rankled was that jibe about lacking patriotism. To some people, that was doubly hard to take from an Australian, although, as I hope I've made plain, that is not an issue for me. It was a remark, however, that set me musing on the very nature of patriotism.

Given that only religion has been responsible for more human misery than the P-word, the logical reaction to being told that you are deficient in patriotism would be to say 'thanks a lot, mate.' Somehow, though, I don't think it's meant as a compliment.

So what is it that's supposed to be missing? Well, we all

have our own ideas of what constitutes patriotism, although it can be as easy to spell out what it isn't rather than what it is. For me, it's nothing to do with Queen or flag. Nothing to do with *Land of Hope and Glory* or *Rule Britannia* but plenty with *Jerusalem*. Nothing to do with colour or race. It's about a deep attachment to the places and people from which you spring – and which you spend half a lifetime getting away from. It's not a love-hate relationship; it's more complex and conflicted than that. And it definitely doesn't consist of giving a dishonestly easy ride to the national team when they screw up.

Nor is the infamous Norman Tebbit 'cricket test' any aid to clarifying the picture, not for me, at any rate. I want England to win at cricket – especially when they play Australia – but not as much as I want Lancashire to win. I couldn't care one way or the other whether England win at football. I want us to win more medals than Australia in the Olympics, but I want England to lose to everyone at rugby union. In some hypothetical game between the England rugby union side and the Australian rugby league team, I would unhesitatingly support the Aussies – something that some of my closest friends find inexplicable and inexcusable, but which others understand instinctively.

Last but not least, I want England or Great Britain (remember them?) to win at rugby league, except that I want the likes of France or PNG to win occasionally, on the grounds that it's good for the game. Australians are, in the best sense, simpler; they just support Australia at everything. The Tebbit Test is no good to me; I might do better at the Ian Sibbit Test, whatever the hell that might consist of. If this is patriotism, it is patriotism of a very confused, inconsistent and selective kind.

And yet I can be moved to tears by English music, the English landscape and the English language in a way I never could by the equivalent from elsewhere. If that equates to patriotism, I've got almost too much of it. As for the connections and disconnections between English and British, let's not even go there.

To try to find the right words to make sense of these ambiguities, in fact, I have to resort to quoting from a song. You wouldn't call Maggie Holland a prolific writer, but every ten years or so she takes aim at some elusive target and hits the mark perfectly. If I've got any patriotic instincts, they are the ones she talks about in *A Place Called England*, which begins in suitably tentative mood:

> *'As I rode out on a bright May morning,*
> *like a hero in a song.*
> *Looking for a place called England,*
> *trying to find where I come from.'*

She reaches a conclusion of sorts
with this:

> *'For England is not flag or empire,*
> *it is not money and it is not blood.*
> *It's limestone gorge and granite fell,*
> *it's Wealden clay and Severn mud.'*

There's not a word there about making up flimsy, fanciful excuses for failing teams, although, funnily enough, June Tabor, who recorded the best-known version of the song, also sings one about a rugby league player, written by Pete Bond, who now lives near Rochdale. It's called *Joe Peel* and, by another co-incidence, it used to be also sung and played rather well by my Sydney mate John's younger brother, before the booze got him. John brought him to Sydney to try to dry him out and he has since confided that repeatedly dragging him out of the Concord Hotel contributed to his own, only recently and partially overcome aversion to the place.

Manly came to A Place Called England and beat Leeds in the World Club Challenge – another blow to national prestige, if you choose to take it that way, but at least it meant we were spared another of Gary Hetherington's Colin Welland-style 'The Brits are Coming' rants. Patriotism, you see, it affects us all in different ways.

Not that it was the easiest of times to be an Australian. From dominating – or at least punching well above their weight – in so many sports, they seemed to be building up a CV as Plucky Australian Losers, or PALs for short.

They'd been hopeless in the Olympics, lost the Rugby League World Cup to the Kiwis, the hybrid footy to the Irish and, whilst I'm not sure what the Wallabies were up to, I don't think it was much good either. Even their irritatingly unstoppable cricket team was showing signs of cracking up, following the loss of one or two useful bowlers, and losing quite regularly to all and sundry, although they showed worrying signs of getting their act together again in South Africa.

The Australian Open Tennis grunted its way through a fortnight with scarcely an Australian contender to be seen – and hardly an Australian spectator there to see them, even in good old sports-mad Melbourne, because it was too hot to watch tennis! How hot does it have to be before swivelling your head from side to side becomes too much like hard work? The temperatures in the mid-forties turned out to be a harbinger of something much, much worse, but at the time they seemed merely to be the world's way of inflicting extra discomfort on them, right across the sporting spectrum.

They haven't quite gone into a national panic, but Australians are asking what has gone wrong with their sport. I'd refer them to that lad in Newcastle who couldn't contemplate walking from leagues club to ground. Multiply him by a couple of million and you have a possible vision of the future that should give us all hope. They already share with us that familiar *bête noire*, The Binge Drinking Culture, and that was what they blamed for Manly spectacularly failing to cover themselves with glory when they returned home as world champions. A boozy party saw one player slap a sponsor and another accused of sexually assaulting a teenage girl. The fact that the second player – Brent Stewart – was the role-model who had been selected as the focus of the NRL's pre-season advertising campaign was an extra source of embarrassment. That and claims, never substantiated, that a Leeds player had been racially abused by opponents at Elland Road. Bad losers we can understand; Manly had turned out to be bad winners.

In the event, Australians had rather more to worry about than a few sporting embarrassments. The boiling mercury at the Open Tennis was, it transpired, a warning of the country's worst-ever bushfires, sweeping through villages on the outskirts of Melbourne and killing more than two hundred people. That's one thing about monsoon rainfall; at least it keeps the flames at bay.

Once again, though, it's the picturesque old gum trees that are some of the villains of the piece. They don't merely burn, they explode – one of the reasons why the inferno spreads at such a speed that you can't even hope to outpace it in your car, always assuming that it hasn't already gone up in flames. It's a reminder that Australia has some wild and intractable party tricks up its sleeve. Just to make sure that nobody took their eye off the ball elsewhere, there was a freakish series of three shark attacks on different Sydney beaches. On the Daintree River, just north of Cairns, a toddler was eaten by a croc – and his parents appealed for the creature not to be put down.

Then there's the economy. The ravening hounds of the global collapse might get to Oz last, but they are definitely getting there. Growth ground to a halt there in 2008 after seventeen years of movement in the right direction and 40 per cent of share values disappeared. As for future prospects, two of the cheerier forecasts I could find on-line were that what remains of the Australian economy is set to unravel as China hits the skids and that the eventual slump will be even worse than America's.

Nor, if you happen to be a rugby league footballer, can you just hop on a plane to England and put your personal finances in order, not if you've been a naughty boy in your past, you can't.

Huddersfield's signing of the serial offender Todd Carney was a predictable first victim of a tougher defensive strategy from the UK Borders Agency, who have proved far more adept at stopping antipodeans than the national team. Mick Crocker's tryst with Hull went the same way, thanks to an assault conviction. During his ultimately unsuccessful wait for a visa, Crocker achieved the distinction of becoming Australian rhyming slang. Instead of saying 'The ref's having a shocker' commentators say 'He's having a Michael Crocker'. It used to be Barry Crocker, the man who played Barry McKenzie in the films, but now, thanks to his shocker with the immigration authorities, it's Mick. That put him up there in the lexicon with Tulsen Tollett, who is rhyming slang for wallet; appropriate for a man with such a well-stuffed one.

Even my new favourite, Greg Eastwood, found his route to Leeds blocked by some driving offences in his youth. I need hardly dwell on the delicious irony of a country which sent Australia so many of its miscreants now baulking at accepting a few back. You could even view it as a way – although an arbitrary and heavy-handed one – of reducing the ridiculous numbers of overseas players in Super League, except that most clubs will simply go out and sign someone else, hopefully after checking that he hasn't got a police record.

The case of Greg Bird is subtly different. Bradford were confident that he would be allowed in, despite an assault charge hanging over him, on the old innocent-until-proven-guilty principle. The British authorities took a different view, but the French cheerfully opened the door for him to play for the Catalans Dragons. He made his first appearance off the bench in March 2009, as opposed to his appearance in front of the bench in April 2009. Just before that, the whole prospect of playing in England became markedly less attractive, for him or any other import, with the stitching up of the loophole that has enabled clubs to pay part of their overseas players' money in tax-free image rights. Some Australian players, or at least their agents, started muttering about going home; no bad thing for anyone in the case of some of the more obvious under-achievers.

There have been some other interesting international movements. At the South Leeds Stadium early in the season, I ran into young Stanley Gene, typically taking the time and trouble to watch three of his *wantoks* – Charlie Wabo, Nicko Slain and Michael Mark – making their debuts for Hunslet against Oldham in the Northern Rail Cup. Presumably none of them had ever been accused of being rascals – as they call delinquents in PNG – in their younger days.

A couple of weeks later, Fiji's Aaron Groom made a televised debut for Sheffield Eagles, alongside another Kumul – the one fated forever to be known as Menzie 'The Man Who Scored a Try Against Australia' Yere. That's nowt – he scored three against Doncaster.

Then there was Ashley Klein. Whilst he was refereeing the World Cup – including, famously, the final – his missus was deciding that she didn't much fancy going back to a Yorkshire winter. Now, one thing I have discovered about this game over the last thirty-odd tear-stained years is that when the words 'wife' and 'homesick' start appearing in the same paragraph, be the husband Brett Kenny, Trent Barrett or Ashley Klein, it only ever ends one way. Sure enough, Ashley is now refereeing in the NRL, who desperately needed reinforcements after their unilateral decision to switch to two refs per game. His duties could include officiating on the Cronulla Sharks, the club coached by his old mate, Ricky Stuart. Ranting Rick's outburst at Klein cost him his other job, with Tim Sheens replacing Stuart as Australian coach. The other candidate was Des Hasler, who was in Leeds with Manly when he learned he had not been given the nod, but didn't seem too bothered.

Of other World Cup coaches, Wayne Bennett stood down from his role as New Zealand's *eminence gris*, Scotland's Steve McCormack lost his club job at Widnes after one match of the new season and John Monie's contract was not renewed by the French. Their feeling was that they needed someone with a little more Gallic *savoir faire*, preferably bilingual, and so appointed Bobbie Goulding, to the astonishment of everybody, including the *enfant terrible* himself. *Sacre bleu* doesn't come close. I'm no linguist, but there is more French in this paragraph than Bobbie has used in his life. *Mon dieu*! Talk about international understanding – there are parts of Widnes where they don't understand Bobbie. But then again, Tom Paine played a pivotal role in the French Revolution and never spoke a word of the language. Plus, Bobbie could have the help of that global diplomat, Garry Schofield.

Tony Smith resigned from what was effectively his day-job as the RFL's technical director – but retained the England coaching job – in order to take over at a struggling Warrington. Out of the mire and into the Wire. Meanwhile, the wheels of England's World Cup inquiry continued to turn and grind exceedingly slow.

Aftermatch: Hong Kong And The Replaying Of Australia

I gave Eamonn McManus his Sevens programme and he confirmed that he had played there for HSBC, back in the days when banks seemed to have a licence to print money, rather than to make it disappear. 'I trust there was some bad behaviour,' he said of my own innocent few days in the former colony – but remember that this is a man who once removed his trousers in the clubhouse at Salford. This conversation and transaction took place before the first Saints-Leeds match of the season. It was a tetchy affair that did its bit to allay any lingering suspicions of excessive mateyness on tour. The most vivid illustration of the barely concealed fury between the two teams came from James Graham, after his team-mate, Maurie Fa'asavalu, had been flattened by Ryan Bailey's shoulder. Other players tend to go red or purple with rage; Graham – cordially referred to as a 'ginger twat' by at least one opponent in this match – goes even whiter, then an icy shade of blue, like a very angry piece of Wedgwood pottery.

It was a game that underlined what I think Terry Matterson had been trying to tell me. Not don't let the rugby spoil the trip, but don't let the rugby spoil the rugby. Super League remains richly entertaining; we don't want to throw it out of the pram just because we've failed to hack it again at international level. It's still a million times more satisfying than the alternatives of football and rugby bloody union; it would just be a blessed relief to scratch this maddening itch of international under-achievement.

That same weekend saw Warrington win for the first time under Tony Smith, who spoke frankly and revealingly about the whys and wherefores of it in a way which prompted some to wonder aloud why we couldn't have him as England coach 'instead of that miserable sod we've got.'

Infinitely more sadly, this was also the same weekend that saw a 20-year-old Wakefield reserve, Leon Walker, die after going into a tackle and collapsing on the field at the Celtic Crusaders.

Fortunately, rugby league, much as it puts us through the mill, is only very, very rarely a matter of life and death; this was one of those days. Walker's funeral was on the day previously set aside for the RFL revealing the findings of its World Cup autopsy, inquest or post-mortem – call it what you will. Not only was that postponed to enable the game to pay its respects, it suddenly seemed like the most inappropriate terminology; no-one had died at the World Cup, only on a rugby field in Maesteg.

When the review of that tournament was unveiled at Red Hall the following week, it was low on any shock revelations. The most interesting aspect was that the majority of the players in the England squad had agreed to be interviewed over the phone by a hired consultant, presumably trained in teasing out the lessons to be drawn from their experience. I'm assured that one of my theories about why the process took so long – namely that the players kept dropping the phone – is not correct.

In essence, the lads blamed themselves for under-performing. No-one blamed the preparation or any extra-curricular factors. Good. Fine. I would expect no less of them. You don't get as far as they have in rugby league by being the sort of person who looks for specious alibis. Nobody claimed that unsympathetic treatment in the media affected his performance.

What, on the other hand, of the great Leeds-Saints schism? Well, players admitted that there were distinct social groupings, but denied that this made any difference on the pitch. That's where they might just be kidding themselves a little. You room with a relative stranger and you not only get to know him, you get to know his mates as well. The whole business of bonding and gelling, if that doesn't sound a bit too DIY, is accelerated – and that's what players say they need more of.

'I'm not saying you're wrong,' says Richard Lewis of this little hang-up of mine, but he's not saying I'm right either. Besides, there was, he tells me, some thought put into it before the World Cup, at least in the case of one notoriously difficult room-mate – no names, no pack-drill – who had to be paired with someone ultra-tolerant if problems were to be avoided.

Seeing that one hundred and forty-four days had elapsed between England losing their semi-final to it being revealed that one player was a smelly sod, this all seemed a little under-whelming. A gross under-statement of the debacle, in view of the time that had passed. No blame had stuck to Tony Smith, who wasn't there anyway – for the understandable reason that subsequent results and performances had shown that there was plenty of work to be done in his day job at the Halliwell Jones. That left much of the coach-speak to be spoken by someone I had never heard of, much less met – the RFL's coaching and performance director, Jon Roberts. Much of the seven-point plan – which, mysteriously, seemed to include a lot more than seven points – flowed straight past me on a tide of well-meaning managementese, but there were things there with which it would be hard to disagree. Getting an elite squad together five times a season was one; giving younger players some touring experience was another. Arguing against those plans would be like arguing against motherhood and meat and potato pie.

There was, however, a fair lacing of the bogus in among the mix. The old chestnut of rule interpretations, which amounts to little more than the unfortunate tendency of Australians to referee like Australians. What do we expect them to do? Referee like Eskimos?

Down And Under

Injuries? Well, it would have been nice to have Sam Burgess, Gareth Raynor and possibly Sean O'Loughlin available, but compare that with the number of players the Kiwis had missing and it looks like grasping at straws.

The most interesting theory, to my mind, was that our players were not wrongly selected or under-prepared, but simply born under the wrong stars. Research has shown that rugby league teams, from junior level right through to Tests, are heavily slanted towards the older lads in each school year. They are that bit bigger and more advanced; they get their noses ahead and they stay there. Those spindly unfortunates like myself, born in the doomed quartile of June, July and August, are left to rot on the vine. The future for rugby league is to 're-engage' – which I sense is going to become a new favourite word – with them. A bit late when the June in question is in 1951.

Meanwhile, Australians of all signs on the zodiac are reacting to the loss of the World Cup by playing rugby league at a tempo I've never seen. The second referee is virtually peeling tacklers off the ruck to ensure that the pace doesn't slacken for a millisecond, which should make the whole issue of interpretations pretty interesting the next time we meet. Setanta cut down their television coverage of the NRL to one match a weekend, because it was too exhausting for British viewers.

Greg Inglis looks big enough to play prop and Canterbury have an 18-year-old centre called Jamal Idris, who is even bigger and seems intent on cramming a whole career into his first few weeks in the NRL. Half aboriginal, half Nigerian, 6ft4, 16st10 and born in July, he was recently suspended for fighting with a team-mate in a car-park. It's the team-mate I'm worried about – that and how we will handle him if he ever makes the Australian side. He is worth mentioning as a reminder that they are still a long way from running out of formidable young athletes, despite the growing couch-potato tendency.

For all the Jamal Idrises coming through the ranks, I still cling to the dream of one day going to Australia with a team of British lads with bad teeth and legs like milk bottles who then proceed to win. I wasn't old enough to even think about a plane ticket in 1970, the World Club Challenge with Wigan in 1994 doesn't really count – although it was fun – and I might have to out-do my dad and live to a hundred to make it come true. But, one day....

Until then, every chance to explore Australia will have its own particular magic. I might finally get to Darwin, or see what that little club competition in Hobart is like, or watch the Stanthorpe Gremlins play the Texas Terriers. I'll almost certainly have a beer or twenty-seven and eat things dragged out of the sea that look like science fiction monsters. I'll have a yarn with some old-timers about what went wrong with the notorious England side of 2008. And, far from letting the rugby league spoil the journey, I'll rely on it to guide me along the way.

The author looks towards a brighter future

POOL ONE RESULTS

Saturday 25th October 2008

ENGLAND..**32**
PAPUA NEW GUINEA **22**
England tries: Gardner (12, 69), Smith (30, 49, 72), Gleeson (57); Goals: Sinfield 4/6.
PNG tries: Griffin (20), Chan (36), Keppa (40), Aiton (75); Goals: Wilshere 3/4.
Attendance: 10,780
at Dairy Farmers Stadium, Townsville

Sunday 26th October 2008

AUSTRALIA **30**
NEW ZEALAND..............................**6**
Australia tries: Inglis (14), Monaghan (29), Folau (47, 80), Slater (59);
Goals: Thurston 4/5, Smith 1/1.
NZ try: Manu (26); Goal: Matai 1/1.
Attendance: 34,157
at Sydney Football Stadium

Saturday 1st November 2008

NEW ZEALAND...............................**48**
PAPUA NEW GUINEA **6**
NZ tries: Ropati (9), Mannering (17, 24), Perrett (34, 71), Luke (56), Fa'alogo (59), Blair (68), Eastwood (77);
Goals: Inu 6/8, Luke 0/1.
PNG try: Moore (48); Goal: Wilshere 1/1.
Attendance: 11,278
at Skilled Park, Gold Coast

Sunday 2nd November 2008

AUSTRALIA **52**
ENGLAND..**4**
Australia tries: Slater (5, 63, 72), Inglis (10, 33, 65), Laffranchi (37, 77), Monaghan (56);
Goals: Prince 8/10.
England try: Roby (20); Goals: Sinfield 0/1.
Attendance: 36,297
at Telstra Stadium, Melbourne

Saturday 8th November 2008

ENGLAND..**24**
NEW ZEALAND..**36**
England tries: Higham (4), Burrow (8, 26), Gleeson (16); Goals: Purdham 4/4.
NZ tries: Vatuvei (14, 47, 55, 78), Hohaia (20), Nightingale (36), Fien (75); Goals: Matai 0/2, Luke 3/4, Smith 1/1, Marshall 0/1.
Attendance: 15,145
at EnergyAustralia Stadium, Newcastle

Sunday 9th November 2008

AUSTRALIA **46**
PAPUA NEW GUINEA **6**
Australia tries: Williams (9, 35, 70), Monaghan (22, 30), Prince (43, 54), Tupou (78); Goals: Thurston 7/8.
PNG try: Yere (72); Goal: Wilshere 1/1.
Attendance: 16,239
at Dairy Farmers Stadium, Townsville

POOL 1 TABLE

	P	W	D	L	F	A	D	Pts
Australia	3	3	0	0	128	16	112	6
New Zealand	3	2	0	1	90	60	30	4
England	3	1	0	2	60	110	-50	2
PNG	3	0	0	3	34	126	-92	0

POOL TWO RESULTS

Sunday 26th October 2008

FRANCE..**36**
SCOTLAND **18**
France tries: Taylor (16), Guisset (28, 74), Wilson (33), Raguin (54), Moly (80); Goals: Bosc 6/6.
Scotland tries: Steel (20), Wilkes (45), Colton (66); Goals: Brough 3/3.
Attendance: 9,287 *at Canberra Stadium*

Saturday 1st November 2008

FIJI..**42**
FRANCE..**6**
Fiji tries: Hayne (6, 70), Divavesi (19), Uate (34, 42, 74), Tora (67); Goals: Naiqama 7/10.
France try: Wilson (30); Goal: Bosc 1/1.
Attendance: 9,213
at WIN Stadium, Wollongong

Wednesday 5th November 2008

FIJI..**16**
SCOTLAND **18**
Fiji try: Tadulala (26, 73), Bukuya (43); Goals: Naiqama 2/4.
Scotland tries: Steel (6), Robertson (40), Wilkes (76); Goals: Brough 3/3.
Attendance: 9,720
at Bluetongue Stadium, Central Coast

POOL 2 TABLE

	P	W	D	L	F	A	D	Pts
Fiji	2	1	0	1	58	24	34	2
Scotland	2	1	0	1	36	52	-16	2
France	2	1	0	1	42	60	-18	2

POOL THREE RESULTS

Monday 27th October 2008
IRELAND..20
TONGA..22
Ireland tries: Blanch (28, 51, 66), Platt (30);
Goals: Richards 2/4.
Tonga tries: Jennings (10), Vuna (35), Uaisele
(58), Tonga (73); Goals: Taufa'ao 2/3,
Williams 1/1, Mateo 0/1.
Attendance: 6,158 *at Parramatta Stadium*

Friday 31st October 2008
SAMOA..20
TONGA..12
Samoa tries: Meli (3), Vagana (16), Utai (38),
Carmont (53); Goals: Roberts 2/4.
Tonga tries: Jennings (20), Leo-Latu (29);
Goals: Williams 2/2.
Attendance: 11,787 *at CUA Stadium, Penrith*

Wednesday 5th November 2008
IRELAND..34
SAMOA..16
Ireland tries: Richards (11, 42, 79), Finnigan
(13), Gleeson (18), Finn (70);
Goals: Richards 5/10.
Samoa tries: Vagana (23), Taulapapa (34),
Solomona (74); Goals: Roberts 2/3.
Attendance: 8,602 *at Parramatta Stadium*

POOL 3 TABLE

	P	W	D	L	F	A	D	Pts
Ireland	2	1	0	1	54	38	16	2
Tonga	2	1	0	1	34	40	-6	2
Samoa	2	1	0	1	36	46	-10	2

PLAY-OFFS

Saturday 8th November 2008
SCOTLAND 0
TONGA..48
(2nd, Pool 2 v 2nd, Pool 3)
Tonga tries: Mateo (4), E Paea (8), Uaisele
(27), Vuna (36, 55), Williams (45), Talanoa
(59), Jennings (80);
Goals: Williams 6/6, E Paea 1/1, Moa 1/1.
Attendance: 5,913
at Browne Park, Rockhampton

Sunday 9th November 2008
FRANCE...10
SAMOA..42
(3rd, Pool 2 v 3rd, Pool 3)
France tries: Guisset (63), Planas (67);
Goals: Bosc 1/2.
Samoa tries: Utai (5), Meli (11), Te'o (23, 47),
Carmont (31), Taulapapa (38), Roberts (60), T
Puletua (75); Goals: Roberts 3/6, Paulo 2/2.
Attendance: 8,028 *at CUA Stadium, Penrith*

SEMI-FINAL QUALIFIER

Monday 10th November 2008
FIJI..30
IRELAND..14
(1st, Pool 2 v 1st, Pool 3)
Fiji tries: Naiqama (2), Uate (29, 77), Bukuya
(55), Hayne (65); Goals: Naiqama 5/6.
Ireland tries: Blanch (7, 78), Grix (36);
Goals: Richards 1/4.
Attendance: 8,224
at Skilled Stadium, Gold Coast

SEMI-FINALS

Saturday 15th November 2008
ENGLAND...22
NEW ZEALAND...32
England tries: Peacock (29), McGuire (39,
74), Gleeson (62);
Goals: Purdham 0/1, Burrow 3/3.
NZ tries: Perrett (9), Hohaia (19), Ropati (22,
68), Harrison (56), Marshall (78);
Goals: Smith 3/5, Marshall 1/1.
Attendance: 26,659
at Suncorp Stadium, Brisbane

Sunday 16th November 2008
AUSTRALIA 52
FIJI...0
Australia tries: Gallen (2), Tate (5, 15), Slater
(8, 37, 49), Thurston (62, 66, 72), Inglis (76);
Goals: Thurston 6/10.
Attendance: 15,855
at Sydney Football Stadium

2008 RUGBY LEAGUE WORLD CUP FINAL

Saturday 22nd November 2008
AUSTRALIA 20
NEW ZEALAND...34
Australia tries: Lockyer (12, 34), Williams
(16), Inglis (65); Goals: Thurston 2/4.
New Zealand tries: Smith (23), Ropati (27),
Hohaia (49, 70 - pen), Marshall (60), Blair
(75); Goals: Luke 3/3, Marshall 2/3.
Half-time: 16-12; Referee: Ashley Klein
(England); Attendance: 50,599
at Suncorp Stadium, Brisbane

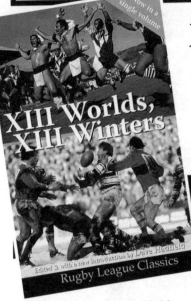

A sports autobiography like no other....

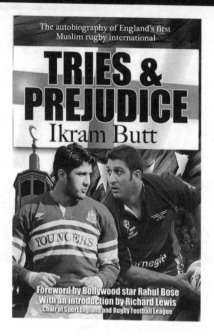

The autobiography of England's first Muslim rugby international

TRIES & PREJUDICE
Ikram Butt

Foreword by Bollywood star Rahul Bose
With an introduction by Richard Lewis
Chair of Sport England and Rugby Football League

In February 1995, Ikram Butt became England's first Muslim rugby international in either code - blazing a trail for British Asians.

Since then, the former Leeds, Featherstone, London, Huddersfield and Hunslet rugby league star has continued to campaign for wider Asian involvement in sport and in 2004 was a prime mover in the formation of BARA - the British Asian Rugby Association. From the start, BARA had a vital social as well as sporting function. How could it not, in the wake of such 'War on Terror'-related atrocities as 9/11, 7/7 and the reported alienation of Britain's disaffected Asian youth?

Now, for the first time, Ikram Butt has his say, telling of his upbringing in Headingley; his own experiences on the wrong end of the law; the potential conflict between personal ambition and religion; racism in sport; run-ins with coaches and short-sighted officials; and, most recently, his regular visits to the House of Commons and pioneering development work in the UK, India and Pakistan.

Tries & Prejudice is by turns amusing, controversial, humane and eye-opening. It provides long overdue food for thought for politicians, the public and sports governing bodies alike.   ISBN 978-0956007537

Available now or coming soon from Scratching Shed Publishing Ltd...